W9-CHS-621

Sexual Predators

Other Books in the Social Issues Firsthand Series:

SOCIAL ISSUES
FIRSTHAND

Sexual Predators

Laurie Willis, Book Editor

GREENHAVEN PRESS
A part of Gale, Cengage Learning

GALE
CENGAGE Learning

Detroit • New York • San Francisco • New Haven, Conn • Waterville, Maine • London

GALE
CENGAGE Learning™

Christine Nasso, *Publisher*
Elizabeth Des Chenes, *Managing Editor*

© 2008 Greenhaven Press, a part of Gale, Cengage Learning

For more information, contact:
Greenhaven Press
27500 Drake Rd.
Farmington Hills, MI 48331-3535
Or you can visit our Internet site at gale.cengage.com.

For product information and technology assistance, contact us at

Gale Customer Support, 1-800-877-4253
For permission to use material from this text or product, submit all requests online at www.cengage.com/permissions

Further permissions questions can be emailed to permissionrequest@cengage.com

Articles in Greenhaven Press anthologies are often edited for length to meet page requirements. In addition, original titles of these works are changed to clearly present the main thesis and to explicitly indicate the author's opinion. Every effort is made to ensure that Greenhaven Press accurately reflects the original intent of the authors. Every effort has been made to trace the owners of copyrighted material.

Cover photograph reproduced by permission of AP Images.

LIBRARY OF CONGRESS CATALOGING-IN-PUBLICATION DATA

Sexual predators / Laurie Willis, book editor.
   p. cm. -- (Social issues firsthand)
   Includes bibliographical references and index.
   ISBN-13: 978-0-7377-4032-5 (hardcover)
   ISBN-10: 0-7377-4032-9 (hardcover)
   1. Child molesters--United States--Case studies. 2. Sex offenders--United States --Case studies. 3. Child sexual abuse--United States--Case studies. 4. Sex crimes --United States--Case studies. I. Willis, Laurie.
   HV6570.2.S53 2008
   364.15'3--dc22

                                      2008002945

Printed in the United States of America
1 2 3 4 5 6 7 12 11 10 09 08

Contents

Chapter 2: Clergy as Sexual Predators

Chapter 3: Sexual Predators Online

Foreword

Social issues are often viewed in abstract terms. Pressing challenges such as poverty, homelessness, and addiction are viewed as problems to be defined and solved. Politicians, social scientists, and other experts engage in debates about the extent of the problems, their causes, and how best to remedy them. Often overlooked in these discussions is the human dimension of the issue. Behind every policy debate over poverty, homelessness, and substance abuse, for example, are real people struggling to make ends meet, to survive life on the streets, and to overcome addiction to drugs and alcohol. Their stories are ubiquitous and compelling. They are the stories of everyday people—perhaps your own family members or friends—and yet they rarely influence the debates taking place in state capitols, the national Congress, or the courts.

The disparity between the public debate and private experience of social issues is well illustrated by looking at the topic of poverty. Each year the U.S. Census Bureau establishes a poverty threshold. A household with an income below the threshold is defined as poor, while a household with an income above the threshold is considered able to live on a basic subsistence level. For example, in 2003 a family of two was considered poor if its income was less than $12,015; a family of four was defined as poor if its income was less than $18,810. Based on this system, the bureau estimates that 35.9 million Americans (12.5 percent of the population) lived below the poverty line in 2003, including 12.9 million children below the age of eighteen.

Commentators disagree about what these statistics mean. Social activists insist that the huge number of officially poor Americans translates into human suffering. Even many families that have incomes above the threshold, they maintain, are likely to be struggling to get by. Other commentators insist that the statistics exaggerate the problem of poverty in the United States. Compared to people in developing countries, they point out, most so-called poor families have a high quality of life. As stated by journalist Fidelis Iyebote, "Cars are owned by 70 percent of 'poor' households. . . . Color televisions belong to 97 percent of the 'poor' [and] videocassette recorders belong to nearly 75 percent. . . . Sixty-four percent have microwave ovens, half own a stereo system, and over a quarter possess an automatic dishwasher."

However, this debate over the poverty threshold and what it means is likely irrelevant to a person living in poverty. Simply put, poor people do not need the government to tell them whether they are poor. They can see it in the stack of bills they cannot pay. They are aware of it when they are forced to choose between paying rent or buying food for their children. They become painfully conscious of it when they lose their homes and are forced to live in their cars or on the streets. Indeed, the written stories of poor people define the meaning of poverty more vividly than a government bureaucracy could ever hope to. Narratives composed by the poor describe losing jobs due to injury or mental illness, depict horrific tales of childhood abuse and spousal violence, recount the loss of friends and family members. They evoke the slipping away of social supports and government assistance, the descent into substance abuse and addiction, the harsh realities of life on the streets. These are the perspectives on poverty that are too often omitted from discussions over the extent of the problem and how to solve it.

Greenhaven Press's Social Issues Firsthand series provides a forum for the often-overlooked human perspectives on society's most divisive topics of debate. Each volume focuses on one social issue and presents a collection of ten to sixteen narratives by those who have had personal involvement with the topic. Extra care has been taken to include a diverse range of perspectives. For example, in the volume on adoption, readers will find the stories of birth parents who have made an adoption plan, adoptive parents, and adoptees themselves. After exposure to these varied points of view, the reader will have a clearer understanding that adoption is an intense, emotional experience full of joyous highs and painful lows for all concerned.

The debate surrounding embryonic stem cell research illustrates the moral and ethical pressure that the public brings to bear on the scientific community. However, while nonexperts often criticize scientists for not considering the potential negative impact of their work, ironically the public's reaction against such discoveries can produce harmful results as well. For example, although the outcry against embryonic stem cell research in the United States has resulted in fewer embryos being destroyed, those with Parkinson's, such as actor Michael J. Fox, have argued that prohibiting the development of new stem cell lines ultimately will prevent a timely cure for the disease that is killing Fox and thousands of others.

Each book in the series contains several features that enhance its usefulness, including an in-depth introduction, an annotated table of contents, bibliographies for further research, a list of organizations to contact, and a thorough index. These elements—combined with the poignant voices of people touched by tragedy and triumph—make the Social Issues Firsthand series a valuable resource for research on today's topics of political discussion.

Introduction

Although it is easier to think of a sexual predator as a stranger who appears out of nowhere, the reality is that most sex crimes are committed by someone the victim knows. According to a 1997 report by the United States Bureau of Justice Statistics, in 90 percent of the cases of rape of a child under twelve years old, the predator was known to the child. About half of the time, that person is a family member. The rest of the time, an adult takes time to get to know a child and gain his or her trust before making sexual advances.

This process is often called "grooming." To the predator, it is a process of getting the young person ready for a sexual encounter. Sexual predators usually place themselves in a position to meet children and teens in a casual way. They might be a teacher, a coach, a clergyperson, a friendly neighbor, or a friend's parent. The predator chooses a child he or she finds attractive. Often they also look for signs that a child is vulnerable in some way—a loner, a child who feels a lack of attention from family or other caring adults, or one who is going through a difficult time for any of a number of reasons.

After selecting a victim (or victims), the predator develops a relationship with the young person by spending time, sharing activities, buying gifts, and gaining the young person's trust. The predator may even become a "friend of the family" and gain the trust of the parents as well. Predators who find their victims on the Internet also spend time becoming "friends" with their victims before arranging an in-person meeting. Sometimes the grooming process takes years before any sexual activity takes place.

By the time the grooming is complete, the victims think of the predators as someone who can be counted on as a friend, as someone who makes them feel special, and often as an object of feelings of emotional love. When the predators begin to make sexual advances, the victims' feelings are usually confused. On one hand, they sense that what is happening is wrong; they may experience emotional and physical pain and discomfort. These feelings become conflicted with their positive, caring feelings toward the predators. Their bodies may also respond physically to sexual touch, which adds to the confusion.

The confused feelings and a sense of their own participation in and responsibility for the sexual activity frequently makes it easy for predators to convince the victims not to tell anyone, to keep "our little secret." The abusive relationship may go on for long periods of time before anyone puts a stop to it.

Charles Christopher, in a September 16, 2002, article in *America* magazine, tells his story about being groomed by a Roman Catholic religious brother, whom he calls "Brother X." Christopher was in his late teens and was a candidate for the Catholic priesthood. The brothers were supposed to teach the candidates and help them grow in their spiritual lives. Brother X noticed Christopher's hesitant and skittish behaviors, correctly interpreting them as an indication that Christopher had had a troubled childhood and was a vulnerable candidate for abuse. Brother X spent two years developing a fatherly relationship of trust and caring with Christopher.

When Christopher turned eighteen, legally an adult but still emotionally a teen, Brother X told Christopher he wanted them to sleep naked together. In his naïveté, Christopher took him literally and thought they would only sleep—another in a series of exercises about trust that they had been participating in together for years. When it became apparent that Brother X wanted more than to just sleep, Christopher was first confused, then paralyzed with fear. Although he ignored the advances and avoided Brother X completely after that night, Christopher still felt a sense of responsibility for what had happened and waited fifteen years before telling his story.

Social Issues Firsthand: Sexual Predators includes other stories similar to Christopher's. In the first chapter, there are stories of victims of a variety of trusted adults. Because abuse by clergy is unfortunately so prevalent, the second chapter is devoted to these stories. The third chapter tells stories of predators who meet and groom their victims online before meeting them in person, and includes some stories about how these online predators are being caught.

SOCIAL ISSUES
FIRSTHAND

CHAPTER 1

Abused by a Trusted Adult

Distinguishing Love and Abuse Is Not Always Easy

Martin Moran

When Martin Moran was twelve years old, his friend George invited him to go along on a weekend trip to a boys' camp in the mountains. The two boys were to help Bob, the owner, do some work around the camp. Moran was thrilled to feel included and enjoyed spending time with Bob, who came across as a caring adult who took an interest in the boys, teaching them about the outdoors, building things, spending time together. On the first night, Bob put his sleeping bag on the floor next to Moran's, and began a sexual relationship that lasted through that summer and the next.

From the beginning, Moran had conflicting emotions about what was happening. At one level he enjoyed the companionship and the sex; at another level he sensed it was wrong. In this excerpt from his book The Tricky Part, *Moran talks about his visits with a therapist years later. Talking about a photo of himself at twelve, he begins to realize that he had been condemning himself all his life for liking, even craving, the attention and the touch he received from Bob. He finally is ready to give his younger self a break for living his life and doing the best he could at the time.*

"I've been at this a long time," [I told Carolyn, my therapist.]

"At what?" she asks.

"Sex that's hidden, fraught. Christ, I've been at it since twelve."

"What happened when you were twelve?"

Reluctantly, I give her a thumbnail sketch. I'm surprised that all these weeks have gone by without my actually talking of it specifically. I tell her I feel like a walking cliché, "another altar boy diddled, blah, blah, blah."

"Do you have a picture of yourself around that time that you could bring in?"

That sounds silly, I tell her. Absolutely maudlin.

"Will you bring a picture of you as a boy next week?"

Using Photos to Remember

Utterly embarrassed, I toted my kid picture to her office the next week. I kept thinking of any number of people, my father, folks at work, who'd scoff at this. The way *I* was scoffing. I was dreading that she would ask me to talk to it or hold it or some stupid thing. The photo I grabbed was one that had followed me around for years. A picture of me standing in a kayak at the edge of a pond. It had been stuck in the bottom of drawers at my various apartments. Tucked in manila folders or between album covers as I moved around California and on to New York. It had come out of hiding one day not long after [my partner] Henry and I met. I gave it to him as a gift because he'd seen it and thought it cute. He framed it and hung it up. I don't recall telling him much of anything about it but that it was at camp in the mountains when I was twelve.

Carolyn asked me to put it down and talk about the time at which it was taken and, strangely, the shift was almost instant. I don't know if it was the photo or being fed up but it was as though a switch got flipped and my body just gave up the ghost. The reversal was powerful, as if the mechanism, the energy, dedicated to burying swapped suddenly to unearthing. My constant reluctance to speak of it, to seriously consider the connection between then and now, lifted. I began to talk forthrightly, for what felt like the first time in my life, about the paper route and George, [who first introduced me to Bob,] the troubled parents and, more than anything, about the counselor. The words tumbled.

After a few weeks of this I blurted out, "I think I'll lose my mind if I say or hear his name one more f--king time. Bob, Bob, blah, blah. I'm wasting time on him. I don't want him in this room or in my life!"

"There's a reason you're talking so much about it, trust your intuition."

Getting to the Bottom

"But why do I come back again to this man?"

"You circle around a story, you come back to it at different points in your life and each time you've spiraled deeper. You're coming at it with more experience, more reflection, till you get nearer the bottom of it."

"But what's the bottom?"

Carolyn tilted her head, smiled.

"There is no bottom, right? Why don't I want to kill him? When I think about the time before I met him, I remember feeling, at the most interior part of myself, really alone and really frightened. About being different, I guess. Being a gay boy, probably. I felt such a sense of doom in that culture. He exploited that and, at the same time, opened something up to me. It was chaos because he was sad and sick. Confused. But he was also a clue somehow. I was drowning in some ways and he was . . . a life preserver."

I looked up at her and repeated *life preserver*. She nodded. She looked at me as though what I'd said was perfectly reasonable. "After all of this, I just called him a preserver," I said.

Facing the Paradox

"It's the paradox. He was destructive. He was a life force. And you reached for that force. In that way he was a life preserver."

"But he was a criminal."

"Yes."

"What he did was wrong."

"Yes."

"In a way I loved him."

"Contradiction is part of the legacy of this. It's part of what grips so tightly. What he did was violent, no question. But that does not erase the fact that he had qualities that you instinctively knew you needed. Wanted. Reached for. Learned from."

Giving Himself a Break

We sat in silence.

"Why do you think you're crying?" she asked.

"Because this is it, the first moment it feels like the rocks are lifting from my chest. Talking about it this way is just a . . . huge relief. A light. I'm the most rabid judge of myself. Punishing myself for going back, for being with him, for admitting my desire. It's almost as if it's the punishment I'm attached to, addicted to. The sense of condemning myself, that kid with the oar, for wanting the attention, the touch, and now I just want to give the kid a f--king break. It's life! He was living his life. He was smart and good and doing his best. He wasn't a bad little shit." I leaned forward on the couch, put my head between my knees. "God, the grip of this is unbelievable."

"What happens when you're a child grips your nervous system."

"What exactly is the grip? Am I trying to re-create the jolt of what happened then? The mother of all orgasms?" I sat back up. "Why do I repeat certain behavior? Why am I talking about it?"

"To get to the other side of it."

"What's the other side? Understanding? Freedom? I've been writing about it like a crazy person. It's the only thing that eases the anxiety. To write and write."

"You once said that your anxiety is like fuel."

"The push, yes. The drive. I feel I have to tell about this. Tell the truth. That I'm *supposed* to. That that's what's meant to be."

"Perhaps it's part of what you're called to do."

"My Great Aunt Marion used to say that. She talked about having a calling. God, if she could see me now in this f--king mess."

"I imagine she'd be very proud."

And I saw Marion's wrinkled face. Saw her countless letters stacked in my drawer. I put my head in my hands. I couldn't stop the tears.

Abused by His High School Teacher

Tom Chiarella

Tom Chiarella attended a Jesuit high school in the 1970s. Early in his freshman year, a French teacher, Mr. Tobin, offered him a ride home. Instead, they went to Tobin's house, where he performed oral sex on Chiarella. Several similar sexual episodes followed. Although the sex itself was not frequent nor ongoing, the teacher continued to torment Chiarella throughout his high school years, sometimes coming off as caring and supportive, sometimes acting as a reminder of what had happened and could happen again.

Now a journalist, Chiarella writes about how deeply his life was affected by this one person. His way of coping was to pretend that nothing had happened and to talk about it to no one. Even after he became an adult, Chiarella kept this part of his life a secret from everyone—including family, friends, and several therapists. Although it is commonly believed that talking about the traumas of one's past is the best way to promote healing, Chiarella opted to keep everything inside of himself for many years, letting healing happen inside himself until he finally felt ready to talk to others about his high school days.

[A]lthough I attended a Jesuit high school, my] French teacher was not a priest. Nor was he really my teacher, at least not that first year; I didn't have him for class until my junior year. He was a little guy named John Tobin, a guy who coached swimming, who advised the French club, who claimed to rehab houses in the city, and who was obviously gay.

He talked to me in the hall on my first day in school, though I can't remember what about. Directions, or instructions. He was generally reassuring. I appreciated it, immediately sensing he was funny, sarcastic, an outsider among the other teachers. He knew my name right away, as if he'd heard of me already. In those first few days, Mr. Tobin was an unexpected undercurrent, a new friend, an adult who seemed to see how dreadfully lost I was. If he had left me alone after that, I would likely not remember him today, save for one piece of advice he gave me the first time I ever talked to him after school. "Chiarella," he said of my shakiness in those first few days, "maybe you had better take up cigarettes." I have to admit that, all things considered, that was pretty good advice.

I always called him Mr. Tobin, even at his house or in his car or when he finally, and absolutely, elbowed me down onto his couch. I still think of him as Mr. Tobin because the title makes him someone I can leave behind, a bureaucrat, an employee, a citizen of another time or place. He wanted me to call him John. I never did. Not once.

I never liked what he did to me, I never wanted it to happen, and truth be told it only happened several times over one year. After that, I found ways to gain distance, to keep him at bay, to sic him on other students. But a few times was enough. It might as well have happened every minute of every day. To say it unmoored me, that it set me floating for several years—leading me to lie to just about everyone I ever cared about—would be about as large and accurate a metaphor as I can muster.

It Began with a Car Ride

It began with a car ride, as it always seems to. I had finished football practice and was trudging across a soggy lawn toward a city bus stop. All around me, the suburban kids were being picked up in handfuls. The sun was low in the sky, I remember, but I wasn't particularly worried about having to take the bus, or even about walking the three miles over the hill to my house. My legs hurt. I felt that my pinkie was broken. Behind me, someone was honking a car horn, but I knew it couldn't possibly be for me. I knew no one at the school, save the few stragglers from my old neighborhood who had ended up there with me, mostly to play football. But when the honking persisted, I turned to find an Opel, driven by Mr. Tobin, filled with guys I later learned were on the swim team. "Ride with us," Mr. Tobin said. "We city kids have to stick together."

They made room for me, and Mr. Tobin turned the car away from the city and began to navigate a route that wound through three suburbs while he dropped four boys at their homes. Each one thanked him casually when he got out; one or two said it was nice to meet me and that they hoped I would swim this year. None of them said much to Mr. Tobin. I remember thinking they weren't very polite and that the sky was thick out there in the suburbs. After the last kid closed his screen door and disappeared into his lamplit home, Mr. Tobin said, "See? They all want you to belong." I had no idea what he meant. I can't say I wasn't anxious about "belonging," but I had never given voice to that worry. Besides, they had hardly spoken to me.

Mr. Tobin never once asked me where I lived. He simply drove straight to his house. During the drive, when it dawned on me that he wasn't taking me toward my house, I thought he was a little obtuse, sort of faggy and self-obsessed, that maybe I was going to have to remind him where I lived. I remember thinking that I wanted to get home to watch television. I remember thinking that I was sick of driving around. I remember thinking that I would never have my own car. I wasn't scared. The truth is, I didn't have a clue.

Raped at the Teacher's Home

Somehow we ended up in his house, with him promising me that he was only going to pick something up, that we'd only be there for a few minutes. He brought out a bowl of olives and a plate of awful-looking vegetables, marinated I think in vinaigrette, and said he had a phone call to make. He walked through the kitchen in his underwear. When he emerged from some back room, he was dressed. He asked me if I was sore from football. Then he wrote a check to the electric company. It was like that. The pace purposeful and slow—obvious, I think now—but his motives easily deniable if it came to that. If he were alive today, I doubt he'd quibble with what I just described. The elements of this world, Mr. Tobin's world, seemed very disconnected to me. One detail would be familiar, part of the sunlit world I already knew—magnets on the refrigerator or a glass of juice—while the next would be odd, an element of seduction—a back rub, exotic food. I was puzzled and, frankly, interested, since it seemed from the moment I'd first known him that Mr. Tobin trusted me somehow, felt that I was special, that I deserved to be shown these new things, to be treated like an adult. I knew that I was supposed to feel lucky.

Ask yourself why you're reading this. Are you just trying to find out what he did to me? Is that all? There wasn't that much to it. In some ways, what he did really isn't the story. It was nothing that hurt me. I won't lie: It felt good, sickening, explosive, bizarre, off-putting. The mechanics of it went like this: At one point he sat down, put his hand under my thigh, and squeezed. I'd told him in the car that I had pulled a hamstring, though I don't think I knew what a hamstring was. I'd just heard about it during football games on television. He rubbed me there, and then he said, "There's something I want to do for you." I resisted, rolled away, twisted back as best I could, but I never ran, or knocked him in the back of the head. I didn't do much more than tell him to stop. It was dark outside now, and it seemed hopeless, and I figured no one would know, and I'd certainly never tell anyone.

He blew me and then he drove me home and I went up into my room and threw away all the clothes I was wearing. I ate dinner with my family. I did my homework. You know how it is. Rape. Sex. Orgasm. After that everything is really loud and out of scale. I managed. The next day I quit playing football.

Pretending to Care

Still, at first, it was impossible to be afraid of Mr. Tobin. He carried on as a friend. He checked in on me all the time at school. He smoothed things over with the freshman football coach. He suggested that I tell people my father made me get a job and quit football, like something out of the Depression. I did that. It was a lie that held for about a month. He urged me to join the swim team and promised me a varsity letter. He seemed to care. He was a jumpy little guy, the kind who could drastically change his appearance from day to day, an expensive tie one day, no socks the next, shaving then not shaving—every morning someone new to deal with. He was puckish and wry. He emanated the air of not giving a damn better than anyone I have ever met. I admired him for it.

So I can't say I was afraid of him, but I avoided him. I jogged home after school. I ducked away whenever I saw his car on the street. I became afraid of the school instead, of the building itself. The only time I ever felt like crying during this whole event was when I pulled up to the school each morning in whatever bus or car I was riding. It was a deep panic, one that I never managed, not with drugs or booze, not for all the while that I was there. In some measure, I felt that grip of panic at the start of every day for four years. Somehow I always made myself put my hand on the bus or car door, pull the handle, step into the constant drizzle.

Running and Hiding

I put an end to it as best I could in December of that first year, which is to say I avoided Mr. Tobin. I hid out. I refused. I ran. I did these things better and faster than I had before. Sometimes he would try to scare me. He once had a priest, a

Latin teacher who hung out with him on weekends, approach me and ask me about my troubles with my father. This man had never spoken to me in my life. He was a gray old guy who knew my name without introduction. I didn't know what he was talking about; I had no troubles with my dad, except that he worked all the time. He asked if I wanted him to call my dad in for a conference. He said Mr. Tobin would be happy to sit in. I couldn't imagine the agenda for such a meeting. More accurately, what I imagined—the meaningful glances, the concerned looks, the endless innuendo—made me feel buried alive. I begged off.

How much do you want me to tell you? How much do you need to know? The facts, the number, the frequency—the math of it all—is still available to me, though I rarely figure it anymore. Back then, though, that's how I spent most of my time—measuring distance, counting days, calculating probabilities. Math. I was a whiz.

Wanting No One to Know

I still know the number. I'll get to that. He said after what would turn out to be the last event that he wanted to introduce me to people but he was "afraid to share." We were at the airport, parked at the end of a runway. He had given me a tiny bottle of Drambuie. Planes descended without warning and landed just beyond us with a screech. Mr. Tobin had some theory about noise and orgasm and lots of jokes about coming and going. I was wickedly afraid of every aspect of his proposition, of the "people" he spoke about and the prospect that what he planned to share was our secret, or, worse, me. He wanted other men to join us, and I refused. If it was just him, just this once, then I felt that I had it under my control. I wanted no one else to know. Not my parents. Not the police. Especially not anyone at that school.

At the end of my first year, I became friends with a priest, to whom I admitted that Mr. Tobin made me "uncomfortable." I remember that his answer made real sense, that I sort of admired it despite everything. "Tom," he said, "people are all different. No matter how strange or funny their behavior is, we have to make room for them. Mr. Tobin does a lot of valuable work for this school and for God." It seemed like something Jesus would say.

Mr. Tobin understood my fear, and he never let up on it. Never. Not for years. Instead of letting it all drift away, letting me forget what had happened, he drew himself closer. At the end of my first semester, he wrote me a card and enclosed a varsity letter in swimming, even though the season was months from being over, even though I never, ever, swam a stroke. Then he changed scores in my French teacher's grade book for me. When I ended the year having failed my final math exam, he went to the office and took me off the list for summer school.

Continuously Tormented

That summer I went to camp four hours north of Toronto. Mr. Tobin showed up and called the camp from town, and I spoke to him from the director's office, the phone like a dead animal in my hand. The camp was on an island. I knew that I couldn't be any safer than that. So I waited him out. That's how it went again and again. Me waiting and not telling.

He always let me know he was there, always suggested that I owed him, always claimed that he had a good heart, a warm spot for me, if only I could get over, well, myself. He reassured me that I wasn't gay. He also insisted that he wasn't, either. I once told him he was deluded. It was the first time I ever used the word. Mr. Tobin told me I had misused it.

Long after he stopped touching me, he played games. He liked to pull up next to me on busy streets, jauntily honking his horn and holding his hand wide open in mock surprise. He often showed up uninvited at my house in the afternoon, claiming he wanted to watch television until my mom got home. He clipped any mention of my father from the newspaper and taped it to my locker. Once he followed my dad around for a day, then reported to me the places he went—squash games, doctors' offices—and the cars he rode in. "Why does your dad limp?" he once asked me in a note he left in my locker.

One July, deep in the hottest days of the summer before my junior year, the time when I basically let myself forget McQuaid [School], I was at work, hosing out a thirty-yard Dumpster, sloshing around in the stench in hip boots, spraying a stream of water into a pile of broken fluorescent bulbs. I remember thinking, This is a sound and smell I will never be able to forget. Looking up from inside the Dumpster, I had the sense that I could not have been more alone. Yet at that moment, Mr. Tobin popped his head over the top of the Dumpster, his hands splayed like a clown's. "Here's your favorite teacher!" he said, his voice echoing above the muck. Startled, I jumped.

He generally had an entourage. Students, swimmers, off-duty priests. I never knew who'd be with him, but it always seemed there was a crowd, that I was surrounded by others, and then suddenly there wasn't, and we were alone and he was driving, or taking me somewhere, somehow keeping me with him, pressing me to relent. Once he showed up at a house where I was baby-sitting with an older kid whom I knew only because he was in student government. They sat on the porch and smoked dope. As Mr. Tobin stole records from the collection that lined the wall, the kid went upstairs to take a pee. Months later Mr. Tobin told me the kid had stolen money from a purse he found up there. "You have to take responsibility for that," he said, but when I cringed, he changed that to "We do." Mr. Tobin suggested that he would split it with me, that we could pay it back together. I told him to forget it. That was my policy. Just forget it.

Incident with Another Teacher

I never knew who was in Mr. Tobin's circle. I never knew who knew about him. About me. The more itinerant priests, the ones who came for a year or two and then left, were the ones he liked best. But it was hard for me to say who was involved in what. As a junior, as my Tobin problems were ceasing, I decided that I wanted to be the announcer for the basketball games, and I had to go to one of these guys to ask. It was one of those deals where I had to screw up my courage, stand in front of his desk, and ask for the job. I felt like a cub reporter going to the editor in chief.

It was a Friday afternoon, in an office in the back of the library. "Of course you can," the priest said, obviously pleased that I was there, pleased that I was asking, that I was so scared. "You come highly recommended. People speak highly of you."

I couldn't imagine that was true. I was as undistinguished a student as any at the school. I lived to be invisible. I was only asking for the job so I'd have an activity to list on my college applications. I shrugged. I figured Mr. Tobin had covered for me yet again.

"Of course," he said, "there is a tradition." I sighed. This was how it went. There was always a tradition, a rite. I wasn't surprised when he rolled back his chair and exposed his casually unsheathed cock, which looked for all the world like the beak of a toucan. I recall that I blinked very hard, so hard that I thought I might not have to open my eyes again. I knew what was happening; I knew where I was supposed to go. But he could see me hesitate, and maybe some look of pain crossed my face. "That's okay," he said, pulling himself in toward the desk. And I answered, "That's okay," and I even waved a little, and I backed out of his office. Nothing was ever said. I knew what I'd seen. I knew what it meant. I knew that it had come from Mr. Tobin, like a message on a forgotten frequency. A month later Mr. Tobin himself handed me the microphone as I was clearing out my locker for the day. There was a lecture,

I'm sure—discretion this, confidence that—but I hardly listened. I knew that stuff by heart.

In some ways, staring at a priest's cock turns out to be a kind of supremely American moment. To my mind, it doesn't seem like the stuff of lawsuits and therapy groups. I speak about it here not because I need to be liberated. Or empowered. Or strengthened in any way. Not speaking about it made me strong for twenty-five years. It just seems like such cheap currency, men and their hard-ons. I'm not kidding myself: It turns out to be not much of a secret after all.

Brother Also a Victim

One spring, while my family and I were vacationing in Florida, I looked up and saw Mr. Tobin through the window of an ice cream shop in Madeira Beach. I recall thinking that I must have been hallucinating, that the sun was creating a lie right in front of me, digging at what scared me most. But there were no lies except the ones I told. Mr. Tobin looked surprised, as did everyone else. He somehow got himself to the house where we were staying, and there was talk of dinner. I retreated to the driveway, where there was an eight-foot [basketball] rim, and dunked my hand numb until he left. It didn't matter, I learned later. Tobin hardly looked at me. He was there for my brother now.

I never knew that until recently. My brother has his own, distinct history with Tobin. Tobin never got to him, though he never quit trying. Tobin stole exams for him, gave him free grades in Spanish, smoked dope with him, got him out of hot water again and again. Once Tobin sat in the front seat of a car and burned the end of his own finger with a cigarette lighter in an attempt to make my brother feel his passion. All this in the hope that Frank would sleep with him. The closer I got to graduating, the more I faded. The only time Tobin really spoke to me during my senior year was when he stopped me in the hall to tell me how "troubled" my brother was. I figured he meant my brother wouldn't play ball, and I told Tobin I didn't give a shit. I really didn't. Either way. I just couldn't afford to care.

Keeping a Secret

Everyone in this country pretty much believes that in order to heal, you have to talk. It's like bearing witness, this opening yourself up, this "forgiving" yourself for what happened to you. You have to tell. You are better for telling. You can help others tell.

I managed this whole thing as a secret from the very start. From the third week of high school through college and graduate school, through years of bartending and tail chasing, of blow jobs in cars and f--king on office furniture, through my marriage and the last days of my divorce, through hundreds of drunken conversations and the deaths of relatives, through promotions at work and the fathering of my two boys, I never told anyone. Not my parents, not my brothers, not my wife, not girlfriends or best friends, not the four therapists I worked with, not the marriage counselor my wife and I saw, not aunts or uncles, not drinking buddies, not my children. That fact doesn't embarrass me so much as amaze me. I'm generally a talker. Silence took some strength on my part.

I suppose there's an easily apprehended psychology to this. You know, the sort of things abuse victims say: The longer you wait to tell anyone, the easier it is to pretend that it didn't happen. That kind of thing. But I don't even call it abuse. I hate that word. I think of it as a kind of chronic, malevolent manipulation. People do this kind of stuff all the time to get what they want. I just wish I'd been in a place where there was more light, less smoke, more exits to take, less grass to cross to safety.

All through high school I had the sense that I could get rid of Tobin somehow if I just said the right thing, promised him something, made him laugh in just the right way. I thought and thought. I calculated and recalculated.

Revealing the Secret

I recall that three years ago [in 2000], after I interviewed [golfer] John Daly for [*Esquire*], I was in Little Rock, killing time before a flight, watching the movie *Magnolia*. In it, a coke-snorting woman lives with the abuse her father wrought upon her—mostly by not living, I guess—and at one point the camera pans away from her to a picture with a little piece of paper taped to it, the words BUT IT DID HAPPEN written on it. It was quite distinct, to me anyway, and I thought I might have been making it up. I turned and looked around the theater to see if anyone else had seen it. I thought of the words as a vision, and I went home and asked my wife to go see the movie with me. I was of a mind to tell her what had happened to me, to introduce the secret to the world. But she hedged, then avoided the subject; eventually she found someone else to go with. She was sick of movies with me. Anyway, when you have managed a lie as long as I had, what good can the truth do you in such small doses? You can't expect to simply dig into the past and heal. Healing is a far grimmer recipe than that.

I teach college now. I watch the sexual-assault support groups rise, bloom, and wither on the college campus where I work. They have slogans, things that ding against the past, against the edge of some of what happened to me. Frankly, I don't like the whole fraternal quality of these groups, the notion of bonds and connections between our separate pasts. I tell my students that the only thing you really own is your past.

About a year ago, I began telling people. For the life of me I can't say what triggered it. I do know that holding it down, keeping the secret in, had stopped bothering me a long time before. I didn't feel particularly wounded, or damaged by it. I simply felt that it was a part of me, a fairly embarrassing part, like some fact about your body—unwanted hair or pudgy cheeks—that you can't change.

The fact that Tobin had died a year prior was undoubtedly part of the equation. But I'm not bent on revenge. I have no real grudge with the school. I know there were teachers who were good to me at McQuaid, but they have mostly faded from my memory. Real kindness is that easily forgotten. I slipped right by them, by my own design, in the manner that I developed, and had they found out it wouldn't have helped me in any way. I learned long ago, blow jobs are pretty transitory, but humiliation is a nightmare that never quits.

Church Members Should Be Trustworthy

Tiffany Allyson

When sixteen-year-old Tiffany Allyson was offered a job in a used bookstore, she didn't hesitate before accepting. Ray, her new boss, was a member of her church whom she had known most of her life. He was almost twice her age. On her first day he began asking questions that made her uncomfortable and giving her inappropriate compliments. Although she was uneasy, she also felt flattered and enjoyed the attention.

It wasn't long before she found herself at Ray's house, where she lost her virginity with mixed feelings of willingness and apprehension. The scenario was repeated over a period of months until a point when she suspected she was pregnant. Receiving no support from Ray, she realized she was being used. In this article, Allyson explains what happened and talks about how counseling and her faith in God played a part in her healing.

I smoothed my skirt, checked my makeup in the mirror, grabbed my purse and breezed out of my bedroom. It was my first day at a new job, and I didn't want to be late. I'd be working in a used bookstore with Ray, a man I'd known from church most of my life.

Ray had asked me to work for him a few Saturdays before, when I was in his store shopping. He had a stack of book posters, but he didn't know where to hang them. I made some suggestions that worked.

"Tiffany," he gushed, "Everyone who's ever met you knows you're an artistic genius, but I think you're an advertising genius, too! This place looks fantastic!" I smiled self-consciously. I was flattered by his compliment. "Seriously, you should work here."

I loved books and was excited about the thought of working in a bookstore. I also thought about how fast I'd be able to save up for a car, and accepted right away.

Uncomfortable Questions

On my first day, Ray taught me how to run the registers and how to catalog new books. Between customers, Ray asked me a lot of questions. He seemed especially interested in knowing about my favorite books and music. Slowly his questions became a little more personal, and then he asked one that seemed awfully private.

"So, Tiffany, are you a virgin?"

"Yes," I answered uncomfortably, "of course I am."

"Going to wait until you get married?"

I nodded.

"Good girl," he said, moving closer and stroking my hair.

The awkward moment ended abruptly when the phone rang. I moved away to answer it, thankful for the distraction.

As my brother drove me home from work that night, I stared out of the window, silently thinking about Ray's question. Replaying the conversation in my head, I decided Ray just wanted to know if I was living up to what the Bible teaches.

That was perfectly innocent, wasn't it?

Questions and Compliments

A few nights later, Ray came from the back office to help me stock books.

"Tiffany, do you have a boyfriend?"

I blushed. "N-no, no I don't."

"But you're so pretty," he smiled. "Those high school boys are just idiots."

I changed the subject with a question about the books. I didn't know what to think—I was a little flattered, but uneasy, too.

This went on for months. Whenever I was the only employee in the store and there weren't any customers around, Ray would come out of his office and talk to me, making comments about how pretty, smart, talented or special he thought I was. Part of me was scared and confused. But another part was like a sponge, soaking in his compliments.

Gradually, the scared and confused part of me became quieter. The fear was overcome by the thrill—a good-looking, single guy was actually interested in me, even though he was in his 30s and I was only 16.

Losing My Virginity

One night, my brother had to work late. "I'll drive you home," Ray offered.

As I threw my backpack into the backseat of his convertible, he said, "Let's stop at my place, OK? I've got some great first editions I know you'll love."

This doesn't feel right. I don't think I should be alone with some guy at his house. But it's just Ray, right? And I don't want to make him mad. I like my job. . . .

Standing at Ray's bookshelf, I looked at the spine on an original copy of Walt Whitman's *Leaves of Grass.* Ray slowly took the book from my hands, leaned over, and kissed me. My heart raced. He smiled. "Wait here."

He walked down the hall and into his bedroom. Then he called my name.

I knew what would happen if I walked down the hall, and I didn't want it to happen. But at the same time, it seemed inevitable. It seemed like it was meant to happen, though everything within me knew it was wrong.

I walked down the hall.

Dealing with Complicated Emotions

After Ray dropped me off at home, I took the longest, hottest shower of my life. Giving him my virginity had unleashed feelings more powerful than I could have possibly imagined just hours earlier.

I'd violated God's laws and everything I believed in. But I was also hurt and confused. Ray hadn't forced me to have sex with him. At the same time, I felt like a victim. I felt like he'd been planning this for a long time, counting on my being flattered and confused. Ray made me feel important and loved, but the price was too high. I felt trapped.

Repeated Encounters

Over the next few months, Ray adjusted my work schedule so I worked more hours. He drove me home afterward, and we almost always stopped at his house. I wasn't worried about getting caught. My mom was too busy to notice what was going on, and she was usually asleep when I got home. My dad wasn't around. Slowly, my mixed feelings became easier to live with.

I hated myself for what I was doing, but I didn't stop.

At church, a few months after that night, my pastor stopped me after service one Sunday. I'd won a Scripture memorization contest. "Tiff, I'm proud you're such a good example to the young women in our church," he said, giving me a side hug. "I wish more of our girls were like you."

I went home and cried for two hours. No one knew what a lie my life had become, and the guilt and shame I'd stuffed away in the corner of my mind suddenly covered me.

Shattered Illusions

The next week, my period was late, and I vomited once before breakfast. I panicked, wondering if I was pregnant. After work, I told Ray about my missed period and vomiting. I'd expected him to be worried, to stop at a grocery store and buy a home pregnancy test. If it was positive, we'd talk about a wedding and how we'd break the news to the people at our church.

His response shocked me. "You're not old enough for an abortion in this state without parental consent," he snapped. "I'll have to go with you. I could pass for your father."

There was no concern for me in his words, just raw fear that the consequences of our actions might catch up with him. I was stunned. Ray had been active in the pro-life movement for years. "I don't believe in abortion," I protested.

His glare terrified me.

It turned out I wasn't pregnant, but the way Ray had reacted shattered my illusions. I'd convinced myself that I was important to him, but deep down, I knew the truth: Ray was using me, and I had given him part of myself that I could never get back.

Anger

Ray ended his involvement with me after about a year, but I kept what had happened a secret for a long time. When I finally opened up to a counselor, I poured out years of hidden shame, self-hatred and anger.

I was angry with God for letting this happen. I was angry at Ray for taking advantage of me. I was angry at myself for needing attention, and for not telling someone what was going on. If I'd just said something—to my brother, my mom, my pastor, anyone—after that first weird comment, the whole situation would have been very different.

Understanding and Healing

My counselor helped me understand that I'd been vulnerable to a man like Ray. I had a normal hunger for male attention—and because I didn't have a good relationship with my dad, I didn't know what kind of attention was appropriate and what was inappropriate. I also didn't trust my instincts. Like many abusers, Ray understood my vulnerability and used it to his advantage.

Now that the ugly episode with Ray is in my past, I've slowly healed and found peace. I no longer blame God for what happened. I no longer blame myself, either. I know God forgives me and loves me. And I now know that God can even use my awful experience to help others. Each time I share my story, I believe it helps bring healing to those who've experienced sexual abuse. I also believe it serves as a warning to those who might be vulnerable to a sexual predator like Ray.

God can take bad situations and redeem them for his glory. I'm grateful for that.

Molested by the Babysitter

Anonymous

In this article, a mom who prefers to remain anonymous tells how her two-year-old son was abused by a babysitter. All names have been changed to protect anonymity.

Alex, the sixteen-year-old son of a coworker, seemed an ideal babysitter for two boys—Charlie, aged eight, and David, aged two. But when David started talking about Alex's penis during a potty-training session, his mom knew something was wrong. She and her husband took David for psychological treatment, where he was able to work through what had happened. David's mom also talked to Alex's mom to let her know what had happened and to suggest that Alex get treatment, too. Later, they received a letter of apology from Alex.

I never saw the signs. I thought everything was fine. But then my toddler told me what had been going on while I was out.

Hiring Alex to babysit my two little boys seemed like a brilliant idea. The 16-year-old son of a woman I worked with, he looked like a stunt double for Brad Pitt in *Thelma & Louise*. As soon as he walked through the door, my husband, Chris, and I took to him. And a male babysitter, I figured, could handle the high-octane energy of Charlie, then eight, and David, two and a half.

It became a ritual for Alex to come over on Saturday night. My boys loved it. Pizza, TV, a cool guy who'll let us stay up late! Chris and I always chatted with Alex and were impressed by how polite and well-spoken he was. And knowing about Alex's difficult life at home—his mother, Susan, had shared stories about her ongoing train wreck of a divorce from Alex's father—made us feel even better about hiring him.

Alone with the Babysitter

One night when my parents were visiting, we went out to dinner while the kids stayed home with Alex. We'd all planned to go to a movie afterward, but at the last minute, my mom and dad begged off and returned to our house. When Chris and I got back later that evening, my mother took me aside.

"Honey," she said, "when we got here, the kids were in the bedroom with that boy, and all three of them had their shirts off. He said he was giving them massages and seemed startled to see us. I don't know, but it doesn't seem right. You hear such terrible stuff these days about what goes on."

I was furious. What was she implying? That I didn't know what kind of babysitter to hire? That I wasn't a good mommy? That I'd invited a pervert into our home?

"Don't be silly," I said in what I am sure was a dismissive tone. "Everything's OK." But it wasn't.

I Learn About Abuse

A few weeks later, I was trying to encourage David to use his potty-chair.

"Mommy, see my penis?" he said happily. "It gets little and big just like Alex's."

I looked at my innocent toddler—the kind of beautiful child absolutely everyone wanted to cuddle and hug.

"David, sweetie, what did you say?"

My little boy repeated the words. I quickly put a fresh diaper on him and raced out of the bathroom to find my husband. Together, we talked to David.

"When did you see Alex's penis?" I asked, trying to sound casual. Perhaps David had simply barged in on Alex while he was peeing.

"He asked me to touch it."

"Did anything else happen?" my husband said.

"He had me lick it."

Older Brother's Perspective

Barely breathing, Chris and I put David to bed. Then we turned our attention to Charlie. "Did anything, uh, strange happen when Alex took care of you?" I asked.

"What do you mean, strange?" he said, not looking me in the eye.

Charlie was in third grade. He'd been drilled by his teachers and by us about "inappropriate behavior." We told him what his brother had said. "Did anything like that happen to you?"

Charlie's first reaction was to be completely grossed out; then, in the way kids have of shutting down just when you want them to talk, he suddenly had nothing to say. Still, he did allow that Alex seemed "weird." Our babysitter apparently preferred to hang out with David in the boys' bedroom while Charlie watched TV in the downstairs den.

Getting Help

It never crossed my mind to call the police. But I knew I had to find a doctor for David—and possibly for all of us—immediately. My first instinct was to talk to my boss. She was not just a sympathetic soul—a mom with two young children—but the wife of a doctor at a prominent hospital. Her calm manner comforted me when I told her what had happened, and she agreed to limit my contact with Susan as much as possible.

By the following day, my boss had found the name of a clinical psychologist, whom I'll call Dr. Green, who specialized in treating very young, barely verbal patients. Dr. Green quickly established that Charlie hadn't been around when the actual sexual abuse occurred; further sessions with him wouldn't be necessary. David, though, would need continuing attention through play therapy.

Dr. Green also told me he wanted to meet with Alex, saying that the boy needed treatment "while there's still time to get him back on track." And the doctor insisted that I tell Susan what her child had done to mine.

Telling the Babysitter's Mother

I dreaded the conversation, but it would have been irresponsible not to have it. If I didn't, how many other kids might Alex go on to abuse? I'd been coached: Repeat, word for word, what David had told us, then ask Susan to call Dr. Green.

Not surprisingly, Susan reacted with indignant denial. "David must have made it up!" she hissed. "Alex would never, ever do anything like this. Get out of my sight." Trying hard to stay composed, I handed her the doctor's number. Then I returned to my office, shut the door, and started to sob.

To her enormous credit, Susan made the call. I don't know where she found the guts, but she set up an appointment with Dr. Green. At work, she and I avoided each other.

Treatment

During every moment with David, I was like a detective, on guard for any sign that he'd been harmed, that irrevocable damage had been done. He struck me as somewhat dingier than usual—and he couldn't have been less interested in toilet training. Otherwise, he seemed like his same, adorable self. The doctor's appointments continued uneventfully.

Until one day. As Dr. Green explained it afterward, while playing with the anatomically correct dolls in the office, David got furious and hurled a male doll across the room. At that point, he and Dr. Green were finally able to talk about what had happened (with some limitations, of course, considering David's age). After two more appointments, the doctor said that as far as he knew, there had been no attempt at penetration—confirming our pediatrician's opinion—and no more treatment would be necessary.

"When he's older, can problems develop from this?" I asked.

"It's highly unlikely, now that he's been treated," the doctor said. "The memory won't be erased, but it will be buried."

"When David's older, should we tell him what happened?" was my second question.

"No," he advised. "It will only be confusing and upsetting."

A Letter from the Babysitter

We never saw Alex again, but we heard from him a few months later. He wrote us a rambling letter filled with apologies: Dr. Green, he said, had encouraged him to put down on paper what he couldn't say out loud. He admitted everything and begged for forgiveness.

As we read the letter, my husband and I wept; when we were done, I crumpled it up and tossed it in the trash. We had no desire to relive the experience by rereading the letter, and we didn't care to write back.

Our lives drifted slowly back to normal. My husband and I each worked out our own feelings about what had happened, and eventually, we didn't need to talk about it anymore. Neither of our sons has ever shown any sign that he remembers the incident.

Susan enrolled Alex in boarding school. She quit her job and moved away.

It's been over 15 years since all this happened, and David, I'm happy to say, has grown into a handsome and charming young man—athletic, talented, a good student. From all I can tell, he is completely normal. He's had a few girlfriends, though he doesn't share many details about his relationships. When I get too nosy, he says with a smile, "I release that information on a need-to-know basis, and you have no need to know."

I had worried that I might become a clingy mom, too protective of David and Charlie. But that didn't happen. What I did become is a mother fiercely proud of her resourceful, independent sons. Whenever I read stories about kids abused by pedophiles, I realize how easily things could have turned out differently.

Parents Miss the Signs of Assault

Patti Feuereisen and Caroline Pincus

When she was nine, Jannie went on a weekend trip with a friend and her friend's family. During that weekend, Jannie was sexually abused by her friend's father. Her mother could tell she was upset when she returned home, but didn't press Jannie to explain why. It wasn't until eight years later when Jannie attempted suicide that the story came out.

This article is by Jannie's mother, who talks about how horrible she and her husband felt when they found out what had happened to Jannie. They felt responsible for not finding out and getting help for Jannie much sooner. Both parents were extremely angry at the man who had abused Jannie. Her father was so upset that he had a heart attack, and died of a second heart attack a few years later at the age of fifty-two. Jannie's mother sank into a deep depression, largely due to the guilt she felt because she was not able to protect her daughter. Rage and anger still consume her. Jannie herself grew up to be a happy adult, although she still carries some emotional scars.

"They were mean to me. They made me do things I didn't want to do." These words will haunt me for the rest of my life.

When my daughter Jannie was nine years old, she went to spend a weekend at her friend Amy's summer home in a chic area of the Jersey Shore, a hundred miles away from our Upper West Side Manhattan home. Jannie had really been looking forward to this weekend away, the last summer weekend before school. We knew Amy's parents and certainly trusted them with the care of our only child, but I hadn't wanted her to go. Before she left, I explained that we could not pick her up if she wasn't having a good time and said that we'd see her in three days. She seemed to understand.

When Jannie got home three days later, she went straight to her room and curled up on her bed. She made me come with her and begged me to stay with her until she fell asleep. Just before she dozed off she uttered these haunting words: "They were so mean to me. They made me do things I didn't want to do." I asked her what they made her do, but she wouldn't answer. She made me check under the bed for "men" and assure her that no one could enter her window (on the twelfth floor!). This was very atypical behavior for Jannie, and I again asked her what had happened, but again she did not answer. I thought perhaps they'd made her eat peas and carrots or something trivial like that. I remember being a bit annoyed and acting abrupt.

Keeping the Secret for Eight Years

Jannie woke up the next morning and went off to school just fine. She seemed all right. And for eight years, she never mentioned that weekend again. I will never forgive myself for being so flip and maybe making her feel that she couldn't talk to me. I can't stop thinking about how I didn't press the issue or beg her to tell me what she meant by those ominous words. It taught me that you should never trivialize what a child says to you.

Jannie's adolescent years were very rocky. She had learning problems and hence some of the other problems that typically result—feeling a bit left out socially, bouts with depression. We were a loving family, but I guess our love wasn't enough to take away Jannie's depression.

Learning the Truth

At age sixteen, Jannie made a suicide attempt and was hospitalized. It was in a family therapy session in the hospital that we learned what had happened to Jannie on that weekend so many years before.

Amy's father had brutally raped and sodomized Jannie. She had just turned nine years old. He told her that if she was a good girl and never ever told anyone, he would not do it again. He told her that it was a very private, important secret, and that harm would come to her family if she told. He pricked his finger with a pin and then pricked hers, and then put their fingers together and explained that this gave them a blood connection. He exploited my poor little girl's insecurity over being adopted. How sick is that? He also said that because she was adopted, she could be taken away from us if she told.

Well, she believed this man, this so-called pillar of the church and community. And she never told until she had to because she was crawling out of her skin.

Jannie's Father's Reaction

When my husband heard Jannie describe the rape, he totally lost it. He made us go to their house straight from the hospital, and he practically broke his hand banging on the door. They let us in, of course, and my husband lunged at the father. His wife and I had to pull him off. At that point, we noticed their daughter Amy crawl under the table. My husband was so enraged he had a heart attack.

After his hospitalization, we began legal proceedings. As helpful and nice as all the police and lawyers were, they made it clear that our daughter would have to testify. Initially, she agreed. But she became so frightened to face Amy's father in a trial that she cut her wrists. At that point, we agreed with the doctors that Jannie could not go through with it.

Jannie also asked us not to tell our friends; she needed her privacy. So my husband and I could confide only in our therapists. Once when we saw the abuser on the street, my husband spat at him. We spent many sleepless nights together trying to figure out how to punish this man. For a few years, my husband would go down to the Fulton Fish Market on Sundays and get some dead fish and put them outside the door of his home. He also sent him threatening letters.

Guilt and Depression

I sank deep into a depression and felt I was the worst mother in the world. I felt doubly guilty because we had adopted Jannie. We were so blessed to have her, and then I did not protect her.

A few years after Jannie's breakdown, my husband died—of a second heart attack. He was just fifty-two years old. I believe he simply couldn't live without seeing justice done. I sometimes wish that I could just kill this horrible man myself. I have had thoughts of cutting off his penis and shoving it down his throat. I am still filled with rage and confusion all these years after my daughter was raped.

The good news is that Jannie is a happy person. She is twenty-seven now and working. She has graduated from college, has friends and a social life, and she is not nearly as scarred from this abuse as I am. Thank God.

Predators Groom Children for Abuse

Anna C. Salter

To help understand how sexual offenders think and operate, Anna C. Salter includes transcripts of several interviews with convicted offenders in her book Predators, Pedophiles, Rapists, and Other Sex Offenders. *The following excerpt is an interview with a man who has admitted to molesting more than one hundred children. He describes the process known as "grooming." The predator develops a relationship with the child, and sometimes also the child's family, before the molestation begins. This man talks about how he chooses a pool of children that he finds attractive, learns about the children and their families, and then selects the child that seems most vulnerable. He becomes friends with the child and with the family. He gains their trust to the point that many parents of molested children continue to refuse to believe he has molested their children, even after his conviction as a child molester.*

A young musician describes to me a process of planning and careful implementation that is anything but impulsive. . . . It is likability and charm that he wields as weapons.

When a person like myself wants to obtain access to a child, you don't just go up and get the child and sexually molest the child. There's a process of obtaining the child's friendship and, in my case, also obtaining the family's friendship and their trust. When you get their trust, that's when the child becomes vulnerable, and you can molest the child. . . .

As far as the children goes, they're kind of easy. You befriend them. You take them places. You buy them gifts. . . .

Now in the process of grooming the child, you win his trust and I mean, the child has a look in his eyes—it's hard to explain—you just have to kind of know the look. You *know* when you've got that kid. You know when that kid trusts you.

In the meantime you're grooming the family. You portray yourself as a church leader or a music teacher or whatever, whatever it takes to make that family think you're OK. You show the parents that you're really interested in that kid. You just trick the family into believing you are the most trustworthy person in the world. Every one of my victims, their families just totally thought that there was nobody better to their kids than me, and they trusted me wholeheartedly with their children. . . .

Choosing Children

Q. At church, you did not molest all the children at church. How would you choose?. . .

A. OK. . . . That's a good question. First of all you start the grooming process from day one . . . the children that you're interested in. . . . You find a child you might be attracted to. . . . For me, it might be nobody fat. It had to be a, you know, a nice-looking child, wasn't fat. I had a preference maybe for blond hair, but that really didn't have a lot to do with it.

You maybe look at a kid that doesn't have a father image at home. You know, you start deducting. Well, this kid may not have a father, or a father that cares about him. Some kids have fathers but they're not there with them. . . .

Say if you've got a group of twenty-five kids, you might find nine that are appealing. Well, you're not going to get all nine of them. But just by looking, you've decided, just from the looks what nine you want. Then you start looking at their family backgrounds. You find out all you can about them. Then you find out which ones are the most accessible. Then eventually you get it down to the one you think is the easiest target, and that's the one you do.

Fooling the Parents

The glint in his eye when he says this is unmistakable. I have shown a film of this man when I give talks, and from the back of a room of 250 people, the glint is still striking. No question this man is sexually attracted to little boys, but it is a hard call to say what matters to him more: the sexual contact with the children or his cleverness in fooling their parents. His cleverness does not stop at getting access; he uses it to protect himself from discovery as well.

Keeping the Child's Trust

Q. How did you keep your victims from telling?

A. Well, first of all I've won all their trust. They think I'm the greatest thing that ever lived. Their families think I'm the greatest thing that ever lived. Because I'm so nice to them and I'm so kind and so—there's just nobody better to that person than me. If it came down to, you know, if it came down to, "I have a little secret, this is our little secret," then it would come down to that, but it didn't have to usually come down to that. It's almost an unspoken understanding.

Q. Do you think any of the families ever became suspicious of you?

A. I'm sure they become suspicious, but that's where I begin my grooming on the family again. . . . If a family becomes suspicious, well, they're not really going to bring it to me, they're going to bring it to the kid first. And the kid, I've got the kid so well groomed that the kid's going to bring it to me and say, "Well, my mom asked me, you know, if you've ever tried to do anything to me or anything like that."

Well, then I begin working on the family by still being kind of nice to them but maybe backing off of that child just enough to where that parent's suspicion gets back down again.

Maybe I'm not with them as much. I won't maybe have as much physical contact. I won't put my arm around the child as much. I'll do everything, whatever it takes to convince that family that there's not a problem.

Fooling the Parents

This young musician admits to more than 100 child victims—I suspect he has many more than that—and out of all these, only one child told and was believed. When the last investigation broke, many of the other parents of children he molested would not even let social services or the police talk to their children. Some of the families still write to him in prison. He could not have been a child molester, and he most certainly never molested their child. After all, nobody was ever better to their child than he was.

When he's done describing all this, he tells me flatly, "child molesters are very professional at what they do, and they do a good job of it." I do not argue with him.

SOCIAL ISSUES
FIRSTHAND

CHAPTER 2

Clergy as
Sexual Predators

Abused by Her Rabbi

Patti Feuereisen and Caroline Pincus

Ivy was a close friend of Sara, the daughter of the rabbi of the Orthodox Jewish congregation that her family belonged to. Ivy would often sleep over at Sara's house. During one of these sleep-overs, when Ivy was fifteen, the rabbi came into the room and abused her while she pretended to be asleep. In the morning, Ivy ran home to tell her parents, who didn't believe her. They took her back to the rabbi's house where Sara also admitted she had been abused by her father. None of the adults believed the girls. Ivy was forced to bury the incident deep inside herself. Her story remained buried until six years later, when a friend convinced her to seek therapy. This is her story as told to therapist Patti Feuereisen.

My family was very religiously observant and went to synagogue regularly. My parents were very close to the rabbi and his family. In fact, my best friend growing up was the rabbi's daughter, Sara. We all lived in a small Jewish en-clave in Borough Park, Brooklyn, and I would often sleep over at Sara's house. Sara was like a cousin to me, and she would come to my house often as well. We went to camp together, we were classmates, and we shared secrets. Sara did not seem close to her father, who was usually working at the synagogue, and because he was so religious, he seemed to be observing one Jewish holiday or another, and was not around much when I was at Sara's house.

One night, when I was about fifteen, I was sleeping over at Sara's. Sara was already asleep when I heard footsteps ap-proaching her room. When I looked up, the rabbi was stand-ing over my bed. He looked at me and whispered "*sha*" ("be quiet" in Hebrew). He was very quiet and sat down next to me on the bed and started petting my hair. I was so nervous, I pretended to fall asleep, hoping that would make him leave.

Before I knew it, he was lying down next to me and rubbing up against me and fondling my breasts. I froze. I prayed he wouldn't notice that I was awake. I began counting to ten over and over again and keeping track of how many times I'd done it. By the time I had counted to ten about twenty-five times, the rabbi had gotten up and left. I just lay there in shock.

I could not sleep and just lay there awake until morning. Sara, on the other hand, appeared to sleep through the whole thing. When we woke up the next morning and Sara asked what I wanted for breakfast, I made up an excuse not to stay for breakfast, and I ran home.

Parents in Denial

When I got home I told my parents right away what had happened. They did not believe me. They said I must have been dreaming, that our wonderful rabbi was not a "pervert" and wouldn't have done these things. They said I should be ashamed of myself for such an accusation. They then marched me over to the rabbi's house, forcing me to tell my "story" to him. Of course, the rabbi denied everything.

Rabbi's Daughter Also Abused

Now comes the twist. Sara must have been listening at the door, because she suddenly burst into the room and confronted her father about how he had molested her for years. In front of me and my family, Sara broke into sobs, saying that she'd been terrified to tell anyone, but that she wasn't going to let him get away with molesting her friend, too. Can you believe the adults didn't believe us, even with Sara there crying and everything? My parents just looked at their beloved rabbi and said, "Rabbi, how could this be?"

In the face of overwhelming evidence, the rabbi continued to deny that he had ever touched either of us. At that point, Sara, who was usually so mild mannered, began to weep uncontrollably. And that's when Sara's father lost his cool and started screaming at Sara violently. It became clear, even to my parents, that there must have been some truth to what Sara and I were saying.

I went over to Sara and hugged her, and she fell into my arms. I kept saying, over and over, "I am so sorry, I didn't know." Suddenly, my one night with her father seemed like nothing in comparison to what he'd done all these years to my dear friend, who had been hiding it the whole time.

Not Allowed to Talk About It

My family took me home and broke off all relations with the rabbi and the synagogue. When I would see Sara in the hallways at school, she'd avoid me. My parents forbade me to go over to her house, and she did not even want to walk home from school with me. My family felt shame for me and asked me not to tell anyone. They finally said they believed me, but they didn't want to talk about it. After a few months, the rabbi's family moved to Israel, and I never heard from Sara again. I also never told anyone about Sara or her father or what he did to me. I just buried the experience deep down inside. I became more isolated. I did not trust anyone. I certainly couldn't count on my parents, so I just kind of withdrew into myself.

When I graduated high school, I moved out and enrolled in college. I limited contact with my family. But six years after this incident, I started having nightmares and becoming depressed. That is when my friend brought me to therapy."

Molested by Her Female Pastor

Allen Salkin and Julie Prey-Harbaugh

From the time she was in the sixth grade, Julie Prey-Harbaugh found friends and acceptance in the youth group at her church. The female pastor, whom she calls "Lizzie," was an important part of this group and made young Julie feel special. Eventually, the two began to spend more time alone together without the rest of the group. A sexual relationship began with a kiss, when Julie was fifteen. Julie was confused by the sexual attention from a trusted religious leader. She had been seeking only friendship and knew that she was attracted to boys. Lizzie convinced her that no one would understand, so the relationship went on and Julie did not talk about it.

Julie eventually got married and believed she had put the episode with Lizzie behind her. But when she heard a speaker at a conference talking about being abused by a pastor, Julie's emotions about being abused suddenly overwhelmed her. She went to counseling, which helped her realize that what had happened had not been her fault. She sought justice through legal channels and through the church, but the results were unsatisfactory. However, she has been able to move on and live her life now, in a healthy relationship with her husband. This is her story, as told to Allen Salkin.

I'm sure you're well aware of the national scandal involving Catholic priests. Well, I was also abused by a religious figure, but my story is somewhat different. Not only am I a woman, but my abuser, a pastor for a United Church of Christ congregation, was female too. At the time, I was a teenager

Allen Salkin and Julie Prey-Harbaugh, "My Female Pastor Molested Me," *Cosmopolitan*, vol. 233, August 2002, p. 154–155. Copyright © 2002 Allen Salkin. All rights reserved. Reproduced by permission of the author.

and didn't realize the horror of what she had done. Eventually, I filed a complaint with the church, but she got off with a slap on the wrist and continues to work with children to this day.

Being Groomed

The actual molestation began when I was 15 years old, but when I look back, I realize that I was being groomed for abuse a lot earlier. I had a great childhood in Pennsylvania, but when I was in sixth grade, I transferred to a new school and the adjustment was hard. I had a real need for friends, and I found them in the coed youth group at my church. We would go bowling and ice-skating and to concerts together, and I loved the companionship. A 27-year-old female pastor, whom I'll call "Lizzie," ran the group. Over the next couple of years, she gradually singled me out for special attention. My parents, who were very religious, completely trusted her, so they were happy to have me go to the church by myself to help her make fliers or plan group trips. She'd also invite me and a bunch of other kids to her house for sleepovers. Eventually, she started inviting just me. She made me feel unique, like I had achieved something by becoming her good friend.

Inappropriate Kiss

One night I was at her house, and we were watching *The Color Purple*. There's a scene where an older woman kisses a younger girl, and I was just sitting there, wondering about what I had just seen, when Lizzie gently leaned over and kissed me on the mouth. I was totally stunned. If it had been a stranger on the street doing something like that, I probably would have punched them, but this was somebody I was supposed to trust, someone I admired, someone connected to God. I didn't know what to do. We watched the rest of the movie in silence.

Then Lizzie launched into a speech. "You're not just a kid to me; you're my friend. I really trust you, and you're so loving and wonderful and kind and the best thing ever," she said, holding my hand. Then she told me, "Nobody else is going to understand it, but I think it's a good thing we're both girls, and you can't really do this sort of thing with boys." Then she led me to her bed and held my hand the entire night as we slept together.

Sexual Confusion

Sleepovers became a regular thing. Lizzie built up the sex part slowly, but within a couple of months, she had touched me everywhere. She'd mostly just kiss me, but on two occasions, she reached under my clothes for my breasts or my crotch, but she stopped short of penetrating my vagina. Afterward, we'd pray together, and she'd thank God for my friendship. Before Lizzie, my only sexual experience had been a few awkward kisses with my eighth-grade boyfriend. I knew I was attracted to boys, but my relationship with Lizzie completely confused me.

And since she always said no one would understand if they knew, I never told my parents anything. Like most victims, I took on a lot of the responsibility for the abuse. It's easier to blame yourself than to think the world is a chaotic place. In some ways, it was actually the ideal teenage romance. She was always giving me gifts like little teddy bears and friendship bracelets made of yarn, and she sent me the sort of flowery love letters that girls would dream of a boy sending them.

I Tell My Future Fiancé

The summer before my senior year in high school, Lizzie left my church to work at a summer camp an hour away, and she stopped calling me. Hurt and confused, I spent my senior year in something of a daze, trying to figure out what had happened. Then I went off to a Christian college, where I started dating a wonderful man named Darin, whom I would marry after graduation. One night at dinner, after I'd been dating him for a month, I blurted out, "I had an inappropriate relationship with my youth pastor." I was in love with Darin, and I knew I was straight, but since I thought the relationship with Lizzie was my fault, I felt I had to admit it to him. (Darin and I had fooled around, but since we were both religious, we were holding off on having sex.) Darin was very understanding and tried to tell me that there was no way I was responsible. The next summer, when I was home and Darin was working 300 miles away, Lizzie called and asked me to go to a concert. When I told Darin about the invitation, he was livid.

At that point, Lizzie was working at a different church, and when Darin came to see me a few weeks later, the first thing he did was drive me there and make me confront her in her office. It was terrible—I wasn't ready. We sat down, and he started ripping into her. But she still had me somewhat on her side, so when she looked at me and said, "Can you forgive me?" my reaction was "I'm so forgiving you. Darin, let's get out of here!" But unfortunately, that wasn't the last I'd see of Lizzie. Eight months later, Darin and I got engaged, and my mother, who still didn't know what had happened, was insistent I invite my former youth pastor to the wedding. It was the last thing I wanted to do, but I was too scared to tell my mom why. So Lizzie was invited, and she actually had the nerve to come to my shower, but not to the wedding itself. I played nice and made small talk, thinking that I had forgiven her.

A Reminder Brings Back the Pain

By this point, I had become a social worker in child welfare, counseling kids in abused homes. But since I still hadn't really dealt with my own abuse issues, the job was too stressful for me. I quit to take a job as a secretary at my church. One night, I was at a youth conference in Saint Louis for work when a woman on stage started talking about being sexually abused as a teenager by her male youth pastor. All of a sudden, wham! I realized that something terrible had been done to me too. I cried my eyes out for an hour, long after almost everyone had left the room.

When I got home, I felt awful for months. My husband and I would start making out, and then I'd suddenly melt down into a horrible mess of misery. I was too sensitive to be touched, even by someone caring, because Lizzie was also supposed to have been caring. I had nightmares of her trying to touch me now and nightmares where I was abusing someone else. I cried all the time, threw things, and broke stuff. It got so bad that some days, I wouldn't make it to work. Darin was patient and tried to help me figure out what to do.

Seeking Justice

After two months of this, I started going to a counselor, who helped me realize that none of what had happened was my fault. But I also wanted to take some control of the situation, so I wrote to the head of the elders at the church where Lizzie currently worked as a youth pastor and told him what she had done. After several letters back and forth, the church ignored my request to turn the case over to law enforcement. So I called the police myself. But they said that the statute of limitations for my case had ended when I was 23, so it was too late to prosecute.

In April 2000, I hired a lawyer, who was able to force the national organization of the church to investigate. I told them that Lizzie had admitted to me that she had abused another girl before me. But all they did was suspend her for a few months and send me some checks totaling $3,000. It was so insulting, I never even cashed them.

At first, I felt so defeated. It angers me that she can live her life, do her work, and put other kids at risk while I have to carry this with me every day. But then I realized that in spite of what happened, I still have a wonderful relationship with my husband, and we're planning on raising a family. I also still have my faith to sustain me. I want to get a doctorate in social work so I can become a therapist and help others deal with sexual and domestic violence issues. And I've also begun working with the support group Survivors Network of those Abused by Priests (SNAP), which is fighting to have statute-of-limitations laws eliminated in cases of child sexual abuse, so I'm still hopeful that somehow Lizzie will be brought to justice. But most important, SNAP helps us remind each other that survivors of abuse can pick up their lives again. It's not easy, but I did it.

Jonathan

Carolyn Lehman

Growing up in a large Catholic family, Jonathan was pleased to be receiving special attention from a priest, Father Jim. But when he was ten, Father Jim forced Jonathan to have oral sex with him and convinced him that the wrath of God would descend upon the whole family if Jonathan told anyone. When the priest suddenly disappeared from his life, some men came to question Jonathan about whether he had been abused, but Jonathan was afraid to tell. He began having migraines and nightmares, and by the time he was in middle school was heavily abusing alcohol, cigarettes, and drugs.

In a project for creative writing class, Jonathan talked about how his brother had saved him from jumping off a bridge. His teacher picked up on the suicidal tone of the essay, and Jonathan started getting the therapy he needed. Now, Jonathan is involved in public speaking, telling his story to other teens and encouraging them to talk about their problems and get help so they can get on with their lives. This is Jonathan's story as told to Carolyn Lehman.

When I was thirteen years old, snorting coke, suicidal as hell, feeling like I had not a friend in the world, if you would have told me "Life gets better. You are here for a purpose, you're gonna help people," I would have told you to go to hell. I'm sorry, excuse my language. I would have said, "You're outta your freakin' mind."

If I'd never talked to anybody about what Father Jim did to me, if I'd never gotten help, the only way I would have been known today is by a headstone. Or maybe my friends would be visiting me in jail.

But now I'm seventeen years old, and I'm known all over the state for my public speaking and for helping other kids.

I grew up in a very strict Catholic family. I'm one of twelve kids, the sixth child down. I have six brothers and five sisters and there's another brother who's adopted. Ten nieces and nephews and two more on the way. My older brothers are all plumbers and tattoo-covered animals. We're just an original bunch of rowdy boys.

Anything that had to do with the church, my family was involved. Until I was in fifth grade, all of us kids went to Catholic school. Me and my brothers were all altar servers. My mom taught religion classes. Both my parents were eucharistic ministers. One year my parents got the Medal of Meritorious Honor from the bishop. We were just totally devoted to the church. The church was our life.

My parents were always there for us no matter what, but with so many kids it was hard financially. The church helped us out a lot. Sometimes they'd bring food over for us. One Christmas they gave presents to my parents to give to me and my brothers and sisters.

A lot of priests were family friends. It wasn't anything out of the ordinary to see a priest just pop in the door to spend time with us or stop over for dinner.

My dad was a police officer for twenty-eight years, always working long shifts, five to seven days a week. When he wasn't working he was sleeping. He had it rough. My mom was just constantly on her feet taking care of us, running us some-where, cleaning the house, getting stuff done for school.

Thursday was the day my mom got to go out. She'd go shopping and we'd order pizza. Father Jim would come over and babysit us, to help her out a little. He'd give us our baths and put us to bed.

When Father Jim came over, I always ran right up to him. My father was my hero, but he worked such long hours I didn't get to see him much. Father Jim was a male figure for me to look up to and I seemed to be his favorite.

In a big family, you don't get a lot of attention. Father Jim gave me his full, devoted attention. He told me he loved me. And I loved having somebody to look up to, somebody who loved me, just me, not the rest of my brothers and sisters. I was proud of the attention.

Now that I look back on it, I'm just starting to realize what was going on then. He did simple things, like he would pull my waistband out and look down my pants. He'd say, "Oh, cool underwear." Maybe I had on Spiderman underwear or something. I was a little kid, eight years old.

I used to sit on his lap when we were watching TV. He would do things like place his hands over my privates. I'm thinking now that maybe that was to test me to see if I was going to say anything. At the time, I didn't think anything about it. A priest was God on earth to me. He couldn't do anything wrong. That's what you grew up knowing as a young child in the church.

I'm beginning to recognize that it was all steps toward taking advantage. Kids just don't realize, because they don't know what sex is. They don't understand when someone's leading up to it. I think parents really need to talk with their children about it. Child sexual abuse is sick, but it's happening, so you have to deal with it.

After a while, Father Jim got more aggressive, more sexual. He started doing other stuff to me, like kissing and touching. He'd do it in his car or in our house when everyone was outside or busy. I had no clue what was going on, but it felt weird.

Then when I was ten I was sitting on his lap in the bathroom. He asked me to look for scars under his private parts. He pulled down his pants and had me look. He was masturbating while I was checking him for, so he said, scars. I told him, "Oh, no, I don't see anything," and stood up, and that's when he forced me to have oral sex with him.

When he was finished he buttoned up his pants and tucked his shirt back in. I started to walk out and he told me, "No, come back." He pulled me down on his lap again and said, "You can't tell anyone about this. If you tell anyone, God's going to hate you. God's going to hate your family. You're going to burn in hell and so is your family."

Being a little kid, having no clue what's going on, I was scared to death. Like, what if somebody finds out? This guy was a priest. I thought he must know what would happen if I told. I believed him. I didn't tell.

That coming weekend, Father Jim was supposed to pick me up to go to the shore with him. It was a three-day weekend, a holiday. And I thought to myself, "What's going to happen? If he takes me away, am I ever going to come back? I don't want to go. I don't want to do this stuff anymore."

I thought if I killed myself and it looked like an accident, nobody would find out. Then my family wouldn't burn in hell. So I planned to hold a steak knife to my heart and run into the wall.

But Father Jim never showed up that morning. He never did show up again. I had no clue what had happened. I thought he just forgot me.

Must have been a couple of weeks later, my mom and one of my older brothers were sitting at the dining room table with a man dressed in a nice business suit. They called me in from outside, where I was playing with my Matchbox cars. Mom asked me if anything strange ever happened with Father Jim, if he'd touched me in weird places. I got scared. I thought, "Oh, my God, they found out! That's it. I'm done for. We're all gonna burn in hell." So I denied it.

I was ten years old. Even after the abuse stopped, I was so worried about it, so confused, I started having migraine headaches and I couldn't sleep through the night. I had these nightmares every night. I'd wake up sweating and crying and wet the bed. That's actually one of the big symptoms of child sexual abuse. I wet the bed until I was twelve years old.

I didn't understand what had happened to me. The schools inform you on sexual diseases, drugs, and alcohol, which is good, but they need to hit a lot of other issues, too, like sexual abuse. They say that one out of every four children is sexually abused. In a class of twenty-four kids, there's a good chance that five or six are abused—or will be.

Because I didn't have that information I started thinking that what happened was my fault, that I did something to bring it on. Like I did something wrong or that I was gay.

When I started middle school and realized what sex was, that's when I really started having a problem with this. Everybody's trying to be the cool one. You know, "I kissed this girl" or "I did this with that girl." But my first kiss was with a man! What happened with Father Jim made me feel like a lesser person.

When I was about eleven years old I started smoking and drinking. It was an unconscious means of coping, but I didn't realize it then. Smoking cigarettes made me feel like, yeah, I was growing up, I was cool, I wasn't a little faggot like I thought I was.

In middle school, my life was hell. I felt I had not a friend in the world. I felt my family hated me. I didn't know what there was to live for. Like, I didn't understand how people could be happy. What was life? Why would you want to live?

Cigarettes, marijuana, and alcohol made me forget my worries, and I thought that was a good thing. I thought that was a great thing! Why would you *not* want to drink and smoke pot? From there, I thought I'd never do anything harder, but I started tripping off acid and 'shrooms and I started snorting coke. Life was a pitch-dark hell to me and doing drugs made me forget that. It made me feel happy.

What I didn't realize was that at the same time it was causing me to have *more* problems emotionally, physically, and education-wise.

It wasn't until eighth grade that the drugs took effect emotionally. I was constantly fighting, always trying to prove that I was a real man, that I wasn't less than anyone else. When I got mad or upset, I'd cut myself with a box cutter. Cut my arms and legs. I don't know why, but at the time it felt good to do it. It was like I was getting rid of the emotional pain by feeling physical pain instead.

I got real suicidal. I took a bunch of pills that I found in the house. I went to bed and planned on never waking up again. It was either live in this hell or move on to the next one, because I knew if I died I'd go to hell. Father Jim told me so. It was just too much to take anymore.

I didn't die, but I got real sick. I didn't tell anyone what I'd done until just last year.

In eighth grade I was really into writing. I was taking a creative writing and public speaking class. We had to write about our hero. I wrote about my brother because deep down inside I had this feeling he had stopped Father Jim from coming to pick me up. He was my hero for that.

So I wrote a story about my brother saving my life, saving me from jumping off a bridge. The teacher already had thoughts that I might be into drugs and alcohol, and now, seeing the suicidal stuff in my story, sent me to the school guidance counselor. The counselor called my parents and set up an appointment for me with a therapist.

I started going to the therapist and telling her about dreams I was having, about somebody chasing me through the woods, and I'd wake up sweating and crying and wet the bed. It was weird, it would happen over and over again. When I told her that, I totally disbelieved that this woman could help me. I never believed in her theory of being able to control your own dreams. I thought it was total bull crap. But it worked.

Her theory was to find out who was chasing me by turning around in the dream and then doing whatever I wanted, like punch him. It didn't work that way. I didn't turn around and shoot him like I wanted to. But I did wake up and see his face and that's when all the pieces just clicked together. I realized the connection between the sexual abuse and the drugs and everything.

So I told my therapist what happened between me and Father Jim. The therapist told my mom. On the ride home my mom said that the same thing had happened to my brother. That weekend when Father Jim was supposed to take me away, my brother had told my parents not to let me go. When they said there was no reason to keep me home, he said, "Yes, there is." And he told them—to protect me. That's why Father Jim never showed up that morning to pick me up. My brother really did save my life.

My parents had reported what my brother said to the church officials. It turned out that the guy in the suit who asked me those questions when I was ten was a church attorney.

This time we decided to go to the police department to file charges. I gave a deposition, told the detective most of what had happened. I didn't tell him the full details. I didn't tell about the oral sex or some of the ways that Father Jim had touched me, because I was embarrassed. I'm a guy and I was thirteen years old. I didn't want them to think I was gay. They didn't have enough to go on and they were busy with other cases. My family just wanted to hurry up and end it, so we settled with the church. The church paid me a large sum of money, and me and my parents had to sign a paper saying I would never talk about it to anyone. The church gave me money in trade for my voice.

I kept quiet for three years—until this past July. That period I kept quiet, I felt like the black sheep at school. I always had problems. It was hard, not being able to tell anyone what happened. A lot of kids didn't understand me. Sometimes, when you're in school, you see these kids that are misfits, these kids that are out there who nobody really takes a liking to, these drug addicts or bad apples. You say, "Ah, that kid's nothing but a piece of crap. That's just how he was raised." But if you look deeper into that person's life, you realize maybe there's something behind it. Maybe he needs help.

This past July I saw a couple of older guys on TV who were abused by priests, guys in their thirties and forties. That's when I realized I wasn't the only one. I'm not alone. And it just happened that these guys were from the same parish as me; they were all from south Jersey.

So I got hold of this group called SNAP, Survivors Network of those Abused by Priests. I started going to the meetings, met other people just like me. It was one of the biggest healing processes for me because—therapist, family, friends—no matter how much they want to help, people do not understand how you feel unless they have gone through it, too. These people became family to me. They knew exactly what I felt. They finished my sentences and I could finish theirs. They were men, women, all ages.

At seventeen, I was the youngest in the group. That was kind of hard, being the youngest. I didn't like the fact that everyone kept telling me how courageous I was for coming out at such a young age. It's different for me than for them because there's so much more support for survivors now. Ten, twenty, thirty years ago, there were no support groups. When people spoke out then, no one wanted to believe it.

In ninth and tenth grade, I'd done some public speaking for PEP—that's Peer Education Program—where high school students who'd gone through drug and alcohol abuse went to talk at elementary schools. Last year, in eleventh grade, I took a whole year of classes in creative writing and public speaking.

When I got involved with SNAP, I decided I wanted to speak out like the older guys. Their reason for doing it is to try to change the church. I wanted to speak out to help other kids. People told me that if I spoke out I might lose the money, and I told myself, "If I help one kid—one kid—that'll be worth it."

SNAP set me up with a reporter from *The Philadelphia Inquirer* and she did a big exclusive on the front page of the Sunday paper. Two days later, we held a press conference.

After that I started speaking in schools. A program called Services Empowering Rape Victims called me. They'd seen me in the newspaper and they asked, "Would you be interested in talking to a couple of people, maybe even giving a speech to a small group?"

So I got hooked up with them and did a speech at a high school in Camden. I walked in and I was the only white person in the room. I was like, "I can't believe I'm doing this," I was so nervous. When I got up to speak, they were all looking at me like, "Who the hell is this kid?"

I told them my story, that I'd been sexually abused. I let the words come from my heart, not a piece of paper. I said, "If you look at life as a road, it has these potholes, the heavy things that happen to you. As I see it, if you try to ignore them or cover them up, not take the time to really deal with them, you're liable to drive back over them and fall in. You've got to take care of them, fill them in, so they don't mess you up." I told them that if I'd never talked to anybody, I would have never gotten help. That's the number-one thing: get help.

When I got done with the speech, everybody stood up. Everybody was in tears and clapping. This one huge kid ran to the front of the room and picked me up and hugged me. It was just amazing. It made me feel so good that I could reach out to other kids and affect them so positively. I decided to do more.

Other teenagers can see that I'm a kid just like them, from an everyday town like theirs, and it hits home. That's when people realize that sexual abuse isn't just a story in a book or a scene in a movie. It's something that happens every single day to people like them.

After the newspaper interview and the press conference, so many kids called me and e-mailed me. People come up to me in public and say, "Hey, aren't you that kid? My friend needs help" or "I know someone who is being abused." Helping other people made me realize there is a purpose in life.

Once I started speaking out and helping people, I realized that this was what I wanted to do. Not for a living, because I'm going to be a pilot, but as my contribution. This is my little bit to make the world better.

When I spoke out, I thought every one of my friends was going to laugh at me. But 100 percent have been right there behind me. Anything I need, anytime I want to talk, they've been there for me. I have their total support.

But you don't have to talk to all your friends about everything. You don't have to get too much into details. It's hard to go into those segments of the past where you're not totally healed. The best person to do that with is a therapist.

When other kids at school found out about what happened to me, a lot of them didn't know how to act. Some people wanted to talk to me. Some kind of ignored me because they didn't know what to say. Some were just uncomfortable with the whole situation.

I remember walking through the hallway at school after the first newspaper article came out. It was my first year in a new school, so I didn't know everybody. I was walking behind this one kid and I heard him say, basically, "I'd have sex with a priest for that much money." Got me real upset, but then I told myself, "You knew people were going to have things to say about this. But the negative you get is nothing compared to the good that comes from speaking out." And it's true, talking about it brought me together with a lot of my friends. It made my life so much easier.

The guy who made that comment apologized to me later. I said, "Don't worry about it." If I hadn't been abused, if I'd just heard this story, I wouldn't know what to think either. I might be joking about it, too. But when people really look at what happened and get some insight, they are more understanding than you would ever think.

There's been a lot of questions from my friends like, "Are you still suicidal?" One friend even asked me if I was gay. And I had these thoughts, too: "If I had sex with a guy, does that mean I'm gay?" But I've found out I'm not gay, I just had these doubts inside me. That's been one of the hardest things to deal with. I mean, I was ten years old, and my introduction to sexuality was with an older male, someone I looked up to.

But being sexually abused by another male doesn't make you gay. It doesn't work that way. You are who you are.

There are so many different kinds of people in this world. One of my family members is gay and I have gay friends. Now I know it's not something to be embarrassed about or ashamed of. And being gay doesn't make someone a pedophile.

I still don't feel comfortable around older men. Maybe it's because I put my total trust and confidence in Father Jim and he took advantage of it. That kind of thing can affect your comfort level and your trust for a long time.

Taking Her Priest to Court

Molly M. Ginty

In this article, "Elizabeth" (her name has been changed to pro-tect her privacy) tells her story of rape and the long road to jus-tice. Elizabeth grew up in a working-class Catholic family and dreamed of someday becoming a nun. She was a lonely child and was happy when the parish priest started paying her special attention. She was happy until he took her to an empty bedroom in an empty convent and raped her. He raped her again at a summer camp and then raped her cousin. Elizabeth stopped go-ing to church and felt that she was responsible for what had happened.

When she was away at college, Elizabeth found out that her sister had been abused by the same priest when she was seven. At that time, Elizabeth didn't have the strength to join her sister in reporting the abuse. Ten years later, Elizabeth read in the pa-per that the same priest was being sued in civil court by sixteen other victims. She, her cousin, and her sister decided to join in the lawsuit. The suit dragged on for eight years before a finan-cial settlement was reached. The six priests involved in the suit were never defrocked and never paid for their crimes.

This is Elizabeth's story as told to Molly M. Ginty, a writer based in New York City.

On a snowy day last March, neighbors in my Connecticut hometown read about the six Catholic priests who had sexually abused 26 children in the Bridgeport diocese for more than 20 years. They read accounts from girls and former altar boys who were assaulted on church grounds, and from one teenage girl who was forced to confess her "sins" afterward. They learned that the church authorities hadn't punished these priests, but instead had covered up their crimes and transferred them to other parishes. The newspaper described the protracted legal battle and reported that the victims' settlement, reached just the day before, was $15 million.

As the the town gossiped over the story of the settlement, I spent the day with my mother. I didn't want anyone to know the secret I had kept hidden since I was a girl. I was one of those children, attacked and raped at the age of 14. I had been waiting for justice for 28 years.

Before my trust, my innocence, and my faith were stolen from me, I had been a devout Catholic. My family was active in the local church. My father, a truck mechanic and skilled carpenter, did construction projects for our priest, while my mother, a housewife, helped decorate the altar before services. My parents sent us to parochial school and to church every Sunday and holy day. We were a run-of-the-mill, working-class Catholic family: Italian father, Polish mother, two sons, and three daughters. I was the shy, quiet girl in the middle— the one with round cheeks and long chestnut hair, who dreamed of someday becoming a nun.

The New Priest Befriends the Family

I was around ten years old when a new priest came to our parish. He was an outgoing man with black hair, a thick mustache, and a gentle sense of humor. When I was 14, he struck up a friendship with my older brother. Once or twice a week, they would go out to dinner or a movie. On weekends, they would head to a cabin that the priest used in New Hampshire. I wanted to go too. I was a lonely kid, and my parents weren't the doting type. We never had enough money to go on vacations, so the idea of a weekend trip was especially intriguing.

I thought my chance was just around the corner when my brother told me one summer afternoon that the priest had said that all of us—my brothers, sisters, and I—might be able to go to New Hampshire together sometime soon.

So I was happy when, a few Sundays later, the priest told my parents after mass that he wanted to spend the afternoon with me instead of with my brother. They knew him and apparently thought nothing of it. He picked me up and drove me to a neighboring town. We were silent during the ride, and I got a strange, uneasy feeling as we pulled up to an empty convent that the parish used for Sunday school.

Rape

As we walked past the storage boxes and up the stairs to the second floor, where the nuns' sleeping quarters used to be, I began to feel nauseous. The priest led me into an empty bedroom and shut the door. Before I could say a word, he pulled off the blue dress that I was still wearing from church and pushed me onto a mattress. He was a huge man—about five feet ten inches tall and at least 250 pounds. When he got on top of me, I remember feeling crushed beneath his weight, terrified because I couldn't breathe. I didn't fight as he raped me. I think I was in shock. All I remember thinking was, please, let this be over.

The next thing I remember is him driving me to a nearby ice cream shop, buying me a cone, and saying, "Don't tell your mother." Then he drove me back to my house. I spent a few hours in front of the television, just staring at the screen. My brothers and sisters drifted through the living room, but I didn't look up or acknowledge them. From that day forward, I learned to survive by blocking out the pain.

My Cousin Is Raped

As promised, we did go to New Hampshire that summer. The priest took a whole group of children to his cabin. One afternoon when the other kids were swimming, the priest asked me to come upstairs with him. When he finished raping me, he called out to my cousin, who was four or five years younger than I and the only other person in the house. When she saw that he was naked, she screamed. As he forced her down on the bed, I started sobbing, grabbed my clothes, and ran out of the room.

I didn't talk to my cousin about what happened. In fact, I didn't discuss the abuse with anyone until years later. Our priest was so well liked in our community that I feared people would never believe me. As the months passed, I retreated further into my own little world—hanging out alone in my room evening after evening or taking walks by myself. I longed to have friends and to be part of a group, but over time, I just stopped trying.

Feeling Responsible

Gradually during the next few years, I stopped attending church. I hated sitting through the priest's sermons and thinking, Why do I have to listen to this hypocrisy? I certainly didn't want him to hear my confession or offer me the Eucharist. Every Sunday, I would lie in bed as my mother screamed, "We have to leave in two minutes!" After a while, she got tired of fighting and gave up.

My schoolwork also suffered. By my junior year in high school, I had skipped so many classes that I was almost held back a grade. Throughout high school and for years afterward, I was haunted by the same thoughts—that I was a terrible person, and that I was somehow responsible for what had happened.

Another Victim

I purposely chose a college on the other side of the country. There, I started seeing a therapist and began to feel better about myself. But in the middle of the semester, my mother called with terrible news. My younger sister, then in junior high, was having serious emotional problems and had just told my mom that she'd been molested by our priest when she was seven years old. I told my mother that the same thing had happened to me, but I didn't go into too much detail. My mom asked me if I was all right, but I felt awkward, fell silent, and was relieved when we finally said goodbye.

The next time I came home from college, my sister asked if I would join her in reporting the abuse to church officials. Saying no to her was the most cowardly thing I've ever done in my life. But I just didn't have the strength to come forward. My sister wrote to the monsignor on her own in 1983. A letter came back several months later asking her to send all correspondence to the church's lawyer. That was it.

Joining a Lawsuit

In 1993, more than ten years after my sister asked me to take a stand, I read in the newspaper that the priest who abused us was being sued by 16 other victims in civil court. I called my sister, and we called my cousin. We all decided to join the lawsuit. We couldn't bring criminal charges because we hadn't reported the abuse within five years after it happened, and the statute of limitations had run out. But under Connecticut law, victims of childhood sexual abuse can press civil charges until they reach the age of 35.

Once others came forward, we learned that six priests from the Bridgeport diocese had molested 26 children between 1972 and 1993. Meeting the other victims in our lawyers' office was difficult, but it helped me realize that I was no longer alone. Together, we sued church authorities for ignoring complaints of rampant sexual abuse and for repeatedly assigning priests to new parishes when these troubling reports surfaced.

For eight years after we filed our case, the Bridgeport diocese tried to sweep the accusations under the rug. At first, the authorities said they had no documentation of sexual-abuse charges, then they refused to submit personnel records for the priests in question. Ultimately, however, their files and other testimony showed that repeated complaints of sexual abuse had indeed been made for years.

No Apology from the Church

In 1996, three years after our initial complaint was filed, a lawyer representing Bishop Edward M. Egan, who had been named to head the Bridgeport diocese in 1988, and Bishop Walter Curtis, the previous head of the diocese, told a judge that if Bishop Curtis were forced to testify, all the "dirt from the distant past would cripple the diocese and its ability to staff its local churches." Over and over, it seemed that maintaining their image was more important to church leaders than helping victims—or making sure these pedophiles didn't strike again.

Church leaders never reached out to us or offered an apology. Mostly they refused to talk about the situation. As late as June 2000, when Bishop Egan left Bridgeport to head the archdiocese of New York, he told a reporter that our suit was giving his priests "a bad rap."

Financial Settlement

With so much resistance from the church, the settlement last March was quite a surprise—and an incredible relief. Coming, as it did, just one month after Archbishop Egan was elevated to cardinal (the highest rank in the Catholic church under the pope), it meant that he wouldn't have to testify in public. Nor, thankfully, would I.

The Bridgeport diocese did finally issue an apology for what it called "incidents of sexual abuse." But Cardinal Egan's personal statement, printed in several newspapers, was disappointingly cold. "Any incidence of sexual abuse is painful for all persons involved," he wrote, "particularly those who are victims of such abuse." And though the six priests involved were suspended, they were never defrocked. They never paid for their crimes.

Moving Forward

I've forgiven my parents for failing to reach out to me more while I was growing up. My brother has apologized for putting me in contact with the priest, although I never asked him if he had any idea what was going to happen to me once he did. I also don't know if my brother was ever molested himself. What I do know is that he feels terrible about what happened, and we are still close. My younger sister went into therapy as a teenager and has stuck with it ever since. Today she's an elementary-school teacher and has two children of her own. We talk often, and I'm very proud of her.

The money I received from the settlement allowed me to pay off my bills and invest for the future. I'm anxious to enter a new stage of my life. At 43, I've never had a romantic relationship. I don't know whether I'll have one in the future, but at the very least, I'd like to get closer to more people. For now, I'm turning to therapy to rebuild my sense of security and trust. I doubt that I'll ever participate in any kind of organized religion again.

It was painful to confront my past, but in the end, I'm glad I came forward. By pursuing this lawsuit, I may have helped prevent what happened to me from happening to another innocent child. And the new bishop of Bridgeport says he will have zero tolerance for priests who commit acts of sexual abuse. That, at least, is a start.

One Act of Abuse Is Too Many

Anonymous

In this article a priest, who chooses to remain anonymous, considers the complicated situation that led to a sexual relationship with a sixteen-year-old boy and the consequences he later faced because of this relationship. During the time he was in seminary, the attitude of the Catholic Church towards sexuality was to ignore it completely. As the sexual revolution of the 1960s and 1970s came about, he had a period of sexual exploration, beginning with masturbation and moving on to sexual encounters with classmates. At his first parish assignment, he became close to a boy he calls "Bill." The relationship was largely based on friendship, but it also became sexual. From the author's point of view, the relationship was mutual, and Bill felt no shame about it. Looking back, he notes that at the time he was not aware that a sixteen-year-old was not legally able to consent to having sex with an older man. His seminary education had not taught him such things. Bill was the only young person he had had a sexual relationship with. Years later, he was informed that Bill was filing a lawsuit against him. He was surprised that Bill was suddenly reporting that he had suffered harm, but he was not allowed to contact Bill to find out what feelings had led to this or to apologize for having hurt him. After six months of treatment, he was sent back to minister in another parish.

Why have priests sexually abused minors? Many of the answers being offered to this question are based on stereotypes, usually the most notorious cases involving serial predators. But these are not the typical cases, most of which go back 20 to 40 years and do not involve many victims. I myself am a priest who committed this crime nearly 30 years ago. This is my story. It is not the whole story of my life, my calling, my spirituality, or the good I have accomplished in the priesthood—just the bare facts that led me to offend, and what happened afterward.

I was a "lifer." I entered minor seminary in the early 1960s at age 14 and went straight on to college seminary, theology and holy orders. We had no seminaries in my diocese, so I boarded at seminaries elsewhere. Discipline in minor seminary was very strict; rules were rigid. Vocations were plentiful, and dismissals occurred regularly, especially for serious offenses like talking back to a priest or leaving the property without permission. Once in a while someone would be dismissed because he was effeminate or it was suspected he was homosexual. Such boys would just disappear without any goodbye or explanation of their going. We only heard rumors.

I had been attracted to girls in grammar school (and I'm attracted to women now), but in minor seminary I never saw any girls my age. The only women were the nuns in the kitchen. Even on summer vacation, seminary rules dictated that we could not go on dates or frequent the company of girls, and my pastor had to sign a document at the end of the summer testifying that I had observed these rules.

Attracted to Boys While in High School

In my junior year, when I was 16, I became aware that I was furtively glancing sometimes at other boys in the dorm as they were undressing. Because no normal male would ever do such a thing, I concluded that this strange habit could only mean that I was homosexual ("gay" still meant "happy" then). As soon as I admitted this to myself, I instantly recognized that I could not possibly discuss this thought with anyone, because if the truth were known I would be abruptly booted out under a cloud of shame and my vocation to the priesthood would be over before it started.

For the next six years of high school and college seminary, I totally suppressed the terrible truth about my sexual orientation—as I knew it then. No one would have identified me as a homosexual—or a heterosexual either. I became the perfect, asexual seminarian who was never troubled by fantasies or masturbation. During all my years of seminary, no issues of sexuality were discussed with us by the priests (only priests were on staff then), except for human reproduction in biology class. Anything to do with sex was a grave matter to be handled by the seminary confessor, a retired priest whose indignant voice roared through the chapel when he scolded a boy for masturbating. I don't blame the priests on the faculty for this. They were good and dedicated people, and they gave us an excellent education in all subjects. They treated sex as everybody did then; it was not a subject for public discussion.

When I was 22, I went to a big seminary for theology. It was refreshing to meet many new people and make new friends. Vatican II had ended a couple years earlier; the windows had opened, and fresh winds were blowing. [Vatican II was a worldwide church council that instituted many reforms and modernizations in the Catholic Church.] The rigid seminary rules were a thing of the past; the atmosphere was relaxed and open. We were treated like adults. We could leave the property anytime we wished, and no one asked where we went. Gone was the prohibition of the college seminary on visiting each other's rooms. I had a sense of freedom that I had not felt before. But I was not ready for it.

This was the end of the '60s and beginning of the '70s, the time of the sexual revolution in segments of the popular culture when "free sex" was touted as normal, healthy and hip. We were part of this young generation and affected by the new ideas. I read a book on situation ethics. The basic theme was that no act is objectively evil; its morality or immorality depends on the situation. I reasoned from this that all sex acts are basically good since God had created us sexual beings, or at least they were morally neutral. They are only evil if they harm someone (like rape or incest or infidelity).

The early '70s was also the time when gays started coming out of the closet in American society. For the first time, people were publicly discussing the very thing that I had kept a dark secret since I was 16. Gays were openly admitting who they were and saying they were proud of it. In the church, hundreds of priests were leaving to marry, and the common wisdom was that celibacy would soon be optional. Things were changing, and I thought that this progress would only continue.

Sexual Exploration

When I began my theological studies, I still had never masturbated, much less had sex with anyone. Then I read a statistic, reported in a newspaper, that 99 percent of adolescents masturbated. I believed it and thought maybe I was strange. So, a period of sexual exploration began. It started with masturbation, and later I had several sexual encounters with classmates in the seminary. It was pleasurable.

I was ordained at 26. My first assignment was to a parish more than three hours distant from my hometown. I went home to visit my family once or twice a month, but I rarely saw my former classmates anymore. I had no friends of my own age in this town. The only time I interacted at any length with other young adults was when I was preparing them for marriage or on occasional visits of classmates to me or I to them. I lived with two other priests, a pastor in his 50s and an associate in his upper 60s. We had little in common.

Working with the Youth Group

A principal ministry assigned to me by the pastor was working with the high school–age youth. I had no particular aptitude or enthusiasm for this work, but I was the new priest and it was expected of me. The other priests certainly were not going to do it. Fortunately, the youth group already existed and was well organized. From the start, I let the teens themselves plan and run things, while I assisted with ideas and support.

One particular boy (I'll call him Bill) took a real liking to me and was always coming around the rectory to see me, talk and kid around. He was also one of the officers of the youth group, so I relied a lot on him to keep things going smoothly. We became pals and did a lot of things together. I had known him a year or so when we first had sexual contact. It started gradually and built up to the real thing. He was 16 then. I had suspected he was gay, and he was. He liked me and admired me. If he felt any shame, it was apparent to no one. We stayed friends and had sex off and on, but that was not the center of our relationship for either of us.

I did not feel guilt at the time, or at least I deluded myself into thinking I actually was doing something good for Bill. I did not want him to live his youthful years suppressing his sexuality as I had done. I wanted him to feel liberated, like I thought I was. I wanted to be a positive role model. I recognize the irony in that now; I didn't then.

Ignorance of Right and Wrong

The factor that contributed the most to my offending was ignorance. I had no knowledge about sexual abuse or harassment. I had no idea that having sex with a 16-year-old was a crime, that he was legally incapable of consenting, or that our sexual activity could cause him any harm in later years. Today, this must sound utterly incredible, but back then these things were not discussed, not in the media, not even in our psychology textbooks. If I had known it was a crime, or if I had known it could cause harm, I would not have done it. I was sexually immature, lacking crucial knowledge and unfaithful to my promise of celibacy, but I was not stupid, reckless or intentionally hurtful.

After Bill went away to college and I was assigned to another parish, we saw each other only a few more times and then gradually lost contact. We were growing up and going our separate ways. Some years later he telephoned, and we chatted a long while. He was living in California; he had a good job and a nice house he shared with his lover, a man his age. He sounded happy.

In my next parish, I was not involved in youth work but was most energized by adult education and faith formation. I was not sexually active. It was not that I was suddenly converted to the position that gay sex is intrinsically disordered. In reality, I was too busy, there were no opportunities for sex, and I'm not sure I would have acted even if there had been. I had noticed a change in myself. I now had begun to think that I must really be a bisexual, because I could not deny anymore that I felt attracted to women.

Platonic Relationship with a Woman

I was working closely in the parish with a religious on the staff (I'll call her Karen). We were planning the liturgies, offering programs in adult education, and leading a prayer group together. We shared similar interests and values. We went to movies and restaurants together. She became my best friend, but our relationship was Platonic. Over time, Karen and I recognized a mutual attraction that had an emotional and erotic dimension to it. We kissed. It could have led to sex, possibly to marriage, but it did not. She was mature in dealing with her feelings about us and where we were heading. We discussed our relationship openly, something that was new to me. I was not good at it, but she brought me along. We worked through it and decided that we both wanted to remain in ministry. We would use the energy of our love in friendship and in service. She is still my closest friend.

I have had no sexual relationships during my priesthood other than the one with Bill. My experience with Karen was the turning point for integrating celibacy in my life in a way that made sense to me. Keeping my promise of celibacy became a matter of personal integrity. I did not want to be living a lie. Although not intellectually convinced of the value of mandatory celibacy, I knew I had to be faithful to my promise for the sake of the people who put their trust in me.

Lawsuit Filed by Bill

Nine years ago, my bishop called with very bad news. He told me that a lawyer for a Mr. N (Bill) was seeking monetary damages for the emotional harm I had caused by abusing him. I was devastated. I admitted it immediately. I wanted to call Bill, to see how he was doing and apologize for having hurt him, but the bishop forbade that. The diocesan lawyer had made it clear that under no circumstances was I to contact the victim, that it would only compound the harm. Later, my own attorney told me that the diocesan lawyer was following standard procedure, because an apology could be used by the lawyer on the other side to get more money from the diocese.

Why did Bill now have this emotional turmoil, I wondered, when he never gave any sign of it before? Did he need the money? Had his lover left him for someone else and he was miserable? Was he trying to protect other boys from me? Did all the publicity surrounding other cases in the news at the time give him a sense of shame he had never felt before? Or, had I really hurt him, and he never got in touch with it until now? I will never know the answer. I wonder whether he himself knows.

Leave of Absence and Treatment

A leave of absence was hastily arranged. I was a pastor by then, and another priest was named administrator. I told the parishioners I was under great stress (which was true) and I needed some time off. They were understanding and supportive. I entered a treatment facility that specializes in the mental health of Catholic priests and religious. While I was there, a cash settlement was arranged by the lawyers representing both parties, and the case was closed.

After the standard six-month treatment, I received positive evaluations from the experts and was judged to be at low risk for re-offending. Following a brief period in a halfway house, I returned to the parish and finished my second term there. The case has not become public.

I am now a pastor in another parish in my diocese. So far, my bishop has not made any move to dump me, as has happened to priests like me elsewhere. I hope and pray he continues to withstand the pressures of the present time, and I pray that Bill has found peace and healing in his life. I want to keep serving the church. I feel I can better make up for the sins of my youth by doing good for other people than by rotting away for the rest of my life in some "safe house."

I worry now whether I could continue in ministry if my bishop were to expose me. I'm sure I would have the backing of my family, friends, mental health professionals and most parishioners. They know I am not a pervert. Shouldn't their judgment matter more to the church than that of the media, the pressure groups and the lawyers who would know nothing of who I really am, other than that I had once offended?

I pray for the church in this time of crisis, especially for healing for priests, victims and the communities affected. I pray also for our bishops, who are overwhelmed now by the turmoil surrounding them. May the Holy Spirit give them wisdom and patience.

CHAPTER 3

Sexual Predators Online

Raped by a Guy She Met Online

Jennifer Leonard

Twelve-year-old Sara didn't have many friends at school. Instead of hanging out with classmates, she spent her time playing games online. She met twenty-three-year-old Jay while playing a game, and they became friends. Sara felt she could confide in Jay, like she could not do with the kids at school. She was living in California, and he was in Michigan, so they communicated by instant messaging and telephone conversations.

When Jay wanted to meet in person, Sara was hesitant but agreed. He told her not to tell her parents because they would not understand. Sara thought they would disapprove of the age difference, so she did not mention Jay to them. When he arrived, Jay took Sara to a hotel room and forced her to have sex with him. Afterwards, he apologized and they went for pizza. He stayed for two more days but there was no more sex, so Sara became comfortable with him again. The same thing happened four more times. Sara was fifteen when she got tired of Jay's control in her life and broke off the relationship. A police investigation ensued, culminating in Jay's arrest. In this article, seventeen-year-old Sara looks back and describes what happened.

Growing up, I never had a lot of friends. In middle school, my classmates teased me for dumb reasons, like the fact that I was tall. It got so bad that in the fall of 2001, I transferred to another school 15 minutes away in Los Olivos, California. But it was just as awful there—the kids were so cliquey. They didn't accept me, and I felt really lonely.

Jennifer Leonard, "My Story," *CosmoGirl!*, vol. 8, December–January 2006, p.102–105.

Meeting Jay Online

After school, I'd go home and play online video games to pass time until dinner. After about three months, I met someone online while playing a game called Age of Empires. His name was Jay, he lived in Michigan, and he was 23. I was only 12, but that didn't bother me. I was just happy to have someone to talk to. Soon we were IMing every day, and in December 2001, I gave Jay my home phone number. He'd call a couple of times a week and give me advice about the kids at school—my mom assumed I was talking to a friend my age. I never thought of Jay in a romantic way; I'd never even dated before. To me, he was just a friend I could confide in.

Our friendship went on for the next year, and in November 2002, Jay suggested we meet up in my town and go to an arcade. That startled me—since he lived so far away, I just assumed we'd never meet. But I didn't want to hurt his feelings so I said okay. That's when he told me not to tell my parents. "They won't understand our friendship," he said. I didn't think much of it. After all, even though *I* was okay with our 11-year age difference, I knew my parents wouldn't be.

Raped in a Hotel Room

A couple of months later, in January 2003, Jay flew to California and I walked to a McDonald's to meet him. As he got out of his car, I felt relieved that he was the same guy who was in the photos I'd seen. He gave me a hug hello and then asked me to go to his hotel room for a minute so he could drop off his bags. When we got in the room, he said he wanted to rest for a bit, so we sat on the bed to watch TV. Then suddenly, he leaned in and kissed me. It was my first kiss, and I didn't expect it, so I pulled away. But he pushed me back on the bed and said, "Come on, I traveled all this way." When I said no, he wouldn't let me go. He tried to convince me this was no big deal as he pulled off my clothes. Then he put on a condom and had sex with me. I was terrified and crying the whole time, but I just tried to pretend like my body wasn't mine and hoped it would end soon. When he was done, we got dressed and he apologized, promising he wouldn't do it again.

Deep down, I knew what he'd done was wrong. But I also felt responsible, like I'd led him on. So I forgave him, and we went out for pizza. Over the next two days, he acted sweet and didn't try anything physical. By the time he left town, I'd convinced myself that he was the nice guy I'd met online—and that what had happened was a fluke.

We went back to IMing and talking on the phone, and things seemed normal again. So a few months later, when he wanted to visit again, I agreed. But as soon as I got to his hotel room, he started kissing me again and saying that without him, I'd have no friends. I didn't want to be alone—but more than that, I was afraid he'd hurt me if I didn't have sex. So I let him do what he wanted. Over the next year, Jay visited me four more times, and each time we had sex.

Breaking Away

It wasn't until April 2004, when I turned 15, that I got fed up with how Jay was controlling my life and got up the courage to stop IMing him. In July, it must have hit him that it was really over and he called my house, angry. My mom answered, but he thought it was me and yelled, "You're nothing but a slut and a whore!" When my mom asked who it was, Jay hung up. She asked me what was going on, but I was too afraid to tell her the truth. But that week, my parents found my IMs with Jay on my computer—so I had to come clean. They were shocked, but they weren't mad at me. They called the police, and after a long investigation Jay was arrested in July 2005.

Healing Process

During the investigation, I was in therapy and realized something: Jay was never my friend. He was a predator who took advantage of me, and he deserved to go to jail. I gave statements against him to a prosecutor and Jay pleaded guilty to his crime. In March 2006, he was sentenced to three years in jail. I wish he'd gotten more time, but I'm trying to put it behind me. I'm home-schooled now, and I'm dating a guy I met through my home-schooling program. I still chat with friends online, but my experience has made me a lot more careful.

In Love with a Predator

Katherine Tarbox

Thirteen-year-old Katie Tarbox met Mark in an online chat room. They began to chat frequently and also started talking on the phone. She felt comfortable with him and felt like she could talk to him about anything. He seemed to her like a very good friend. At first, he told her he was twenty-three then later said he was really thirty-one.

This excerpt compiled from the chapters "Apart" and "Together" from her book, A Girl's Life Online, *takes place about six months after she and Mark met online. Katie, who lived in Connecticut, was planning on participating at a swim meet in Texas, and Mark asked if he could fly there to meet her in person for the first time. Although Katie expressed some hesitation, it was overridden by her sense of excitement at finally meeting "the love of her life" face to face. Mark phoned Katie's room when he arrived at the hotel. It was late in the evening, and Katie had given up waiting for him and gotten ready for bed. She went to his room to meet him, still dressed in her pajamas with her mom's raincoat over them. She expected to meet a friend and was not worried about how she was dressed. It was when he began making unexpected sexual advances and did not respond to her declaration of love that she started to become aware that she had been wrong about the whole relationship. (Subheads have been added to this material that were not included in the original book.)*

[Mark asked,] "What if I came to Texas?"

At first, I didn't know what to say.

"Katie, what if I were to fly there from California so we could meet?"

"Oh, I'm not sure it's the right time or place. It's a national [swim] meet, you know. I'm going to be under a lot of pressure."

"Katie, are we ever going to get together?"

"What do you mean?"

"Are we just going to talk forever? This has been going on for six months, you know. I thought we had a connection, that you wanted to see me as much as I want to see you."

"But I do. . ."

"All right, then you're probably just nervous. That's understandable. But believe me, it's okay. I'm just going to come, and I'll see you there. Even if it's just an hour, that's okay. We deserve it, don't you think?"

I couldn't answer.

"Katie? Do you want to see me?"

"Yes."

"All right then. It's settled. I can't wait."

He asked if he should stay at the same hotel my team had booked. I said yes, but I told him I had never seen the place, so he should not expect much. I didn't know what kind of hotels he was used to staying in, or whether he knew how to rough it.

"There's probably going to be five hundred girls and their coaches in this hotel," I warned. "It could be really noisy."

"I can handle it, no problem. I really want to finally meet you."

"Me too."

Excited About Meeting Him

The day before I left I was excited, as if it were Christmas Eve, or the day before my birthday. It was a Monday night. I didn't have to swim that day, because they rarely made us swim before a large meet.

So after doing a little homework, I began to lay some clothes out on my bed. My family always says I overpack. I am not quite as bad as [my stepfather] David, who once packed seven shirts for two days, but I can overdo it. This time I had an excuse. The winter climate in Dallas is iffy. It could be cold or warm. It could rain or be perfectly sunny. That meant I had to bring many types of clothing, because I always felt it was better to be safe than sorry.

Eventually, the wardrobe I chose covered my bed, and that didn't include shoes. I packed jeans, sweaters, shorts, dresses, you name it, I had it in there. I wanted to have choices when I got to Texas. And though I do think about my clothes a lot, I honestly didn't think about what I would wear when I first met Mark. I knew that given the way he felt about me, any-thing—even jeans and a T-shirt—would be fine.

It was about ten p.m. when Mark called. I was excited to hear his voice. In my mind he was no longer just an on-line buddy that I met in a chat room. He had become the love of my life. I loved the way he talked. It was soothing and sweet. I lay back on my bed, feeling comfortable, happy, *loved.* . . .

Waiting in the Hotel

[The next day] in the hotel room I shared with [my friend] Ashley I waited and waited without a word from Mark. I tried to watch TV to pass the time. I think it was a news show like *Dateline,* but I'm not sure now. I heard voices coming from the set and saw that there was some sort of picture, but that was all. I was lost in imagining Mark's voice, his words, and his face as the door to one of the hotel's rooms swung open.

By 8:45, which felt like 9:45 to me, I was convinced that he had changed his mind and was not coming. I was disap-pointed. I had thought about his arrival constantly for over twenty-four hours.

I was so sure that he wasn't coming that I decided to put on my pajamas and go to bed. Ashley wanted to go to sleep too, so we both got ready. While she went to the bathroom I changed into a white camisole, a white Gap T-shirt, and then my flannel polar bear pajamas. They were my favorite pajamas, a Christmas gift from my grandparents when I was in the fifth grade. Because I had worn them so much the flannel was rubbed smooth from wear, so smooth you couldn't even tell it was once flannel. There was a hole under one armpit and a hole in the left leg, but I still wore them. I loved them. Feeling cozy and safe in my familiar pajamas, I got under the covers, turned out the light, and rolled over to sleep. It was 9:15.

Mark Finally Arrives

It was 9:37 when the phone rang. I mumbled a hello and the phone cord became tangled around my hand.

"Hello," he said, with a hint of excitement in his voice.

"I thought you weren't coming, why were you late?" I talked softly since Ashley was awake and in the bathroom.

"I missed my connection. Actually, it was pretty close. I was running through the airport and got to the gate just as the plane was leaving. There wasn't another flight for a couple of hours."

"Well, you're here now."

I sat up from the bed and leaned forward to the phone. I dangled my feet and curled the phone cord as it moved over them.

"So when am I going to get to see you?" asked Mark. "Can you come down now?"

"I guess I can come down for a quick hello."

"I'm on the ninth floor, room 938."

"I'm on the eleventh."

"Well, get yourself down here."

"Okay."

On My Way to Meet Him

I hung up the phone, got out of bed, and stood there for a moment to think about what I was doing. I was in my pajamas. I knew I wouldn't look my best, but I didn't think he should care. We were friends. More than friends, actually. It shouldn't matter how I dressed.

An hour earlier my mother had left her raincoat in our room as she was going out to the grocery store to buy some breakfast food for the morning. Now that I was dashing out, I decided to grab the coat to cover my pajamas. As I did, Ashley came out of the bathroom.

"That was him, wasn't it?" said Ashley. "I knew he'd convince you to meet in person. He's here, isn't he?"

"We're just going to say hi. That's it."

"Katie, I don't think . . ."

"He's in 938. If you get worried, you can call me down there."

When I went to the door, Ashley jumped in front of me. I couldn't do anything else but laugh because I thought she was joking. But she insisted that I stay and braced herself with one hand on the door handle and the other pressed against the door frame.

"You can't go see this freak," she said. "I won't let you."

"He's not a freak. Let me out."

I knew she was just ignorant, unable to understand a mature relationship. I looked at her and tugged on the door. She was not going to stop me, and she knew it, so she let go. Neither of us said anything as the door swung closed behind me.

I paced the hall as I waited for an elevator. I couldn't imagine what was taking so long. There were six of them, after all. Then I heard the chime, which was not so different, I guess, from the chime that announces "You've got mail" on AOL. The door opened. I got inside and pressed the button. Nine. The doors closed, and I took a deep breath.

Meeting Mark

I stood outside Mark's door for a minute, looking at the PRI-VACY PLEASE sign on the knob, steadying myself. I was now about to meet the man I loved. He knew so much about me, but also very little. He knew my stories, my struggles, and my accomplishments. But he knew none of the thousands of little things that become clear when people meet in person—every gesture, turn of the head, change in the voice. I felt strange, almost disoriented, and extremely nervous. I lifted my hand and tapped gently on the door.

I was expecting to meet a trim man, based on his photo, but when Mark opened the door I was absolutely shocked by how short he was. Since I am short, I always expect that people are the same height as I am, or taller. Mark was tiny. And he was the scrawniest man I had ever seen.

Later Mark would say he hugged me at the door, but I can't remember that. It could have happened, but I wouldn't bet money either way. He walked over to the sofa and invited me to join him there. Instead, I went to the chair that was facing him. I sat down and looked at him more carefully.

He was wearing dark jeans, the kind of deep blue denim that you expect to see on a cowboy, and a shirt with vertical stripes of maroon and cream against a blue background—navy blue to match the jeans.

I would have stopped thinking about how he looked if it hadn't been for the shoes. They were hideous. They were white canvas with a chunky rubber heel, very feminine. They might have been somewhat stylish for a girl at the time, but I couldn't imagine a man wearing them. I couldn't stop staring at his shoes, even after he started talking.

"How was your trip?"

"Okay, okay." I couldn't think clearly enough to say anything more.

"God, I can't believe I missed that connecting flight. We were late taking off, and then they circled the airport for what seemed like forever. The pilot said they would hold the planes for people with connections, but of course they didn't."

"Uh-huh."

"I'm hungry. Are you hungry? I haven't had anything all day, really. Why don't you just go up and put on some jeans and we can go out?" he said.

Go out? It was close to ten o'clock. I had to wake up at dawn. And besides, I was fourteen years old. There was no way I could just leave the hotel without someone knowing.

"Mark, I ate, and besides, it's pretty late, don't you think?"

"But there's no room service after ten, and I'm really starving."

I just looked at him and he finally gave in to the fact that I wouldn't go no matter what he said. I began to feel a little uncomfortable. Nervous.

"I've been in worse hotels," he said, suddenly changing the topic. "But they're pretty cheap here. I mean, come with me and look at this bathroom."

Starting to Feel Uncomfortable

He got up, and so did I. He waited until I started moving and then placed his hand on my back to direct me. No one had ever steered me like that before. And with his touch I suddenly realized how uncomfortable I felt with him.

This wasn't at all what I had expected. We were such good friends—more than friends—on the Internet. No one had ever made me feel safer and more at ease. But here, in his presence, I was anxious and confused.

"Look at this," Mark said once we were in the bathroom. "There's not even a soap dish, and the towels are so thin they might as well be made of paper."

I couldn't look Mark in the eye; in fact, I couldn't look at him at all. I glanced into the large mirror that was behind the sink instead, and felt a shiver of surprise to see my reflection joined by his. Then I gazed down at all the toiletries on the counter. He had a large silver can of Gillette shaving cream, which seemed awkward to me. He also had a large bottle of cologne.

"Smell this," he said. He picked it up and waved it under my nose.

"Yuck, Mark. I can't stand the smell of cologne."

"Katie, just stand still," he said. He put his hands on my shoulders and then looked past me into the mirror. "I thought you would be taller."

I wanted to say to him that I thought he would be a lot taller himself. But I didn't. "Well, I told you I was short" was all I could mutter.

Mark wanted to show me a new watch that he had bought and he rushed out of the room to get it. I followed him and he gave it to me to hold. The weight and the quality made me think it was solid gold.

"Is it real, I mean, solid gold?"

"Of course. How could you even ask?"

He grabbed my hand to admire my own Seiko watch. As he did, he glimpsed my necklace. It was a fourteen-karat gold necklace with a piece of jade that was carved into the Buddha of laughter. He took the Buddha in his hand.

"This is beautiful, Katie. I really like it."

"My grandmother gave it to me. She brought it back from Thailand."

"I love your shoes, too."

They were simple Birkenstocks, the most common style sold, in the most common color.

"And your eyes . . . so pretty."

Mark stepped a little closer, looked into my eyes, and then gently touched my shoulders, my waist. No grown man had ever inspected me like this before, and it made me self-conscious. I was glad that my pajamas covered me so well. I nervously played with my necklace. He sat down on the sofa. I stood for a moment, then glanced at the television.

"Do you think it's possible to get a VCR in this hotel?" I asked. "Ashley and I brought some videos."

"You could probably rent one," he said, then added quickly, "Come sit here on the sofa."

Without thinking, I did what he said and sat down on the opposite end of the sofa, facing him.

"I need a haircut," he said.

"No, you don't," I said. He seemed feminine, worrying so much about his hair.

"Give me your hand," he said. "I can read your fortune."

I played along, giving him my right hand. He turned it over so he could examine the lines that hold the answers to life's mysteries. He began to stroke the life line.

"I can see right here that you are going to have a long, rich life."

The First Kiss

He continued to caress my hand. It felt comforting. But when I tried to pull back, he held on harder. It became more difficult to concentrate on what we were supposed to be talking about because my attention was fixed on his hands touching mine. There was a strength in his hands that was different from mine. His skin was smooth. The small lines seemed more defined, and the hair on the back of his hands was more conspicuous.

I had never felt a man's hand in this way. I never held David's hand. And it had been years since my grandfather had stopped taking my hand, the way grandfathers take the hands of their little granddaughters.

"Katie, I have been thinking about you all day," he said softly. "And I have been thinking about doing this."

This. I knew what "this" was. I knew he wanted to kiss me. I felt a shiver of anxiety, not because I didn't want him to, but because I was so inexperienced.

I didn't move as he leaned forward. I closed my eyes and could feel the warmth of his face as it came close. I wanted to be a good kisser. Not because it was expected of me. Not because I was swept up in passion. I wanted it because of what I felt for Mark, and because I didn't want to say no.

Our lips met and I felt his tongue slip under mine. It was fat, and wet, and warm. I felt a few stray whiskers that he had missed with the razor, and suddenly I realized that this was a grown man who was giving me my first real kiss, not a fuzzy-faced teenager, not someone my own age.

Unwelcome Advances

Something inside me snapped. Now I didn't want this at all. But I couldn't speak. I hesitantly pulled away. He lifted my shirt and grabbed my breast. Now the strength of his hands meant something different. It hurt, but I said nothing. I felt completely numb. And then I thought, Do I owe this to Mark?

"C'mon sweetie, relax."

He tried to reach into my pajama bottoms through the fly opening. I pulled his hand away. He did it again, and I pulled his hand away again. Then he pushed down on me hard, letting me know he would not be resisted again.

Instead of being angry and shouting at him to stop it, I was confused and speechless. Mark was supposed to be better than this. He was supposed to be patient and kind and generous. He was supposed to care about me. Now it was clear that he obviously wanted me to have sex with him. That was what this meeting was about. He moved on top of me. I wondered what a mature person, a woman, would do, but I could think of nothing.

"We could have such a good future," he whispered.

"How do you know?"

"A little bird is telling me."

It was silly and I laughed nervously. It was then quiet, and I had a moment to think about how much I really cared about him.

"I love you," I said.

I told him because I wanted him to know how much I looked up to him. He was everything that I thought a person should be. And when he said nothing in response, I knew that I was wrong about him, about myself, about love, about everything.

Fooled by a Police Officer

Sandy Fertman Ryan

Brittany thought she was a savvy user of MySpace. She knew to delete messages like, "I need nude pictures of you." But she didn't think twice about posting her real name, age, school, and photo online. All her friends did it.

When she received a message from Matt, who said he was nineteen and new in her town, he seemed harmless. They developed an online friendship. Then, Brittany was invited to participate in a forum of teens teaching adults about MySpace. She was surprised to see that it was to be televised on Dateline NBC. *She was even more surprised when she and the other girls were asked if they knew Matt. All of them had been talking to him online. They were introduced to Detective Frank Dannahey, who had been chatting with them online. He was doing an experiment to learn about how easy it was to con teen girls online. Brittany talks about how it felt to discover she wasn't as safe as she had thought she was. She went home and removed a lot of personal information from her MySpace page and began speaking at other high schools about Internet safety. This is Brittany's story, as told to writer Sandy Fertman Ryan.*

MySpace is great. You basically have your own website, and people read your stuff, look at your photos and ask to be listed as your "friend"—which means they can go to your personal pages. The more friends you have, the more popular you feel. Most pages have photos, quotes, likes and dislikes, hobbies, anything and everything you want to put on there. Although MySpace doesn't require you to write your age, city or real name, practically everybody does it because, if you don't, you could look boring and no one would want to be listed as your friend.

Sandy Fertman Ryan, "I Thought I Was Chatting with a Teen . . . ," *Girl's Life*, vol. 13, August–September 2006, p. 89. Copyright 2006 Girls' Life Acquisition Corp. Reproduced by permission.

When I first started using MySpace, I submitted everything about myself—my town, school, age, photo and interests. I thought it was literally "my space." I never told my mom I was on MySpace because I didn't know what she would think. At the time, I wasn't close to her. I figured since all of my friends were doing the exact same thing, it had to be safe. Even so, I did get unwanted sexual solicitations, like this guy who messaged me, "I need nude pictures of you." I deleted messages like that, but I didn't think it was a big deal. I thought I had handled it. Looking back, though, I can't believe I was so naive. Right before I started using MySpace, there had been seven incidents of girls ages 12 to 17 in my town who were sexually molested through meeting people on MySpace. I even knew one of the girls! I just believed nothing bad would ever happen to me.

A Message from Matt

After two months on MySpace, I got a message from a 19-year-old named Matt who said, "I'm new in town and looking for friends." He said he lived at the nearby college but had a cartoon character instead of a photo posted. He asked to be added as my "friend," and I accepted him after I saw that all the friends listed on his profile were people I knew. After chatting with him every night for two weeks, I thought Matt was cool and pretty decent. It wasn't like a crush or anything, but he felt like a good friend. We talked about everything: baseball, my favorite coffee shop and lots of other stuff that made me feel like we had so much in common. I never even considered that he could be making me believe we were so much alike because he was reading about me on my personal page.

I became so comfortable with Matt that I told him we should meet sometime—still, I wouldn't have gone by myself. I was brought up to never meet strangers, so I don't even know why I suggested it. I guess it was because I felt I could trust him—and I thought MySpace was safe.

Meeting the Real Matt

One day, my mom told me a couple of my friends and I were randomly selected from our school to teach adults about MySpace. On the day of the event, we all walked into this room at school—and we were shocked to see nine TV cameras set up. Our interview was to be televised on *Dateline NBC*. The interviewer asked us about MySpace and whether we talked to strangers. He asked, "Do you think you'd know if a stranger were trying to con his way into your life?" We all said, "Probably." He said, "Well, there's this new kid in town named Matt. Do you know him?"

My jaw dropped, and my heart was pounding. The interviewer then asked if we'd like to meet Matt, and we said "No!" We were so scared since all of us had been talking to him online. But then he said, "Matt's just outside the door." This man in his 40s wearing a badge walked in, and I was like, "He's a cop!" Matt sat down, introduced himself and told us he was using us as an experiment to see how easy it was for teen girls to get conned online. I thought, "How could I have been so stupid?" It really was the biggest shock of my life. When the interview was over, I thought my mom would kill me. But when she saw me, she broke down in tears. This whole experience has made us closer and, now, I really have no secrets from her. That night, I went home and removed all the "friends" I didn't know. I also took off my city, school and photos. Since then, I speak at high schools with Matt, who is actually Detective Frank Dannahey, about the dangers of meeting people online. It's great to teach other kids how to be safe online. The point is not to be afraid to use the Internet. It's to learn to protect yourself.

Posing as a Teen to Help Stop Predators

Julie Posey

When she was a young teen, Julie Posey was the victim of a neighbor who was a sexual predator. As an adult, she has used her Internet skills to help in tracking predators online.

In this excerpt from her book They Call Me Kendra, *she describes how she created the personality and personal story of her online character, Kendra, to be attractive to predators, and how Kendra needs to behave in order keep her own actions within legal limits. Posing as a teen in chat rooms, Kendra agrees to meet the predators in person. When the predator arrives at the scene of the "date," he is met instead by a law enforcement officer.*

I set out to create what would later become the online personality by which I was known among both sex offenders and law enforcement. I created the guise of a lonely and vulnerable teen needing attention. Everything about the character I created to use as my online alias was created for an essential reason, and was not just randomly produced or selected. My purpose was not to get as many sex offenders arrested as possible, but to have high-quality, prosecutable cases to present to law enforcement. I wanted to see as many convictions as I possibly could, so I was very methodical in each aspect of the creation of the character I would portray. It had to be believable, and the details had to be such that they would stand up in court.

I chose to name my character Kendra. There was one way to spell it, it was easy to remember, easy to pronounce, and it was a popular name. Kendra's age was 13–14 years old. If it was likely that there would be Federal charges, she was thirteen. There are Federal statutes in place which allow for more serious charges and longer prison sentences if the sexual crime is committed against a child under the age of fourteen. Many states have "age of consent" laws, but rarely can a child under the age of fourteen legally consent to having sex with an adult.

Kendra was an only child in a single parent home. She was not doing well in school, and didn't have many friends. The average child molester is not looking for the most popular kid at school who is excelling in every subject. He is looking for a young person who has a physical or emotional need that he can fill. Kendra had also been suspended from school for fighting, had outbursts of anger directed at a teacher, and other minor disciplinary problems. This kept me from having to tell an offender the name of Kendra's school, and assured me that the sex offender would not be hanging out in front of a middle school stalking a girl who resembled Kendra's description.

Kendra's mother often worked for a temporary agency, filling in all over town wherever she was needed. She frequently accepted assignments without notice and worked varied schedules. This allowed me to have some flexibility with law enforcement. If a needed officer was tied up in court all week, that was the week Kendra's mother was always home and Kendra could not meet anyone in person. When the officer became available, Kendra's mother would suddenly accept an assignment and not be home.

The teenager that I would portray was not sexually active, or even out looking for sex. She was a virgin. Many sex offenders prefer to be the one who teaches a child about sex. I also wanted to avoid any questions about entrapment issues and knew that an inexperienced teen would lack the basic knowledge of sex to even have such a conversation.

Before going online to pose as Kendra, there were some other things I had to keep in mind. Kendra could not ask for pornography to be sent to her (as it is a felony to possess child pornography), so I disabled attachments in my e-mail software. Also Kendra could not ask to meet anyone or be the one to bring up the topic of sex.

I posted the paper with Kendra's profile on the wall next to my computer and I became the child who agreed to meet many sex offenders in person. They would not actually be meeting me, but would meet a police officer or other law enforcement agent instead, when they chose to cross the line between fantasy and reality with the intention of having sex with a child. I sat in the darkest, shadowy corners of the Internet and listened to sex offenders tell of their plans to rape, sodomize, molest, and sexually assault children. I did this so that a real child would not be violated and would never have to meet the person that I was in communication with.

I Worked as Live Bait to Help Catch Sexual Predators

Jennifer Leonard

Twenty-year-old Emily was frustrated because her size and looks made her appear much younger than her real age. These characteristics worked to her advantage when she was offered an acting job for an NBC series called To Catch a Predator. *They needed an actress who was over eighteen, but appeared to be younger. Her job was to pose in front of a Web camera pretending to be a young teen chatting with a predator. When the predator showed up to meet her in person, he was met instead by a television camera and law enforcement officers. This article is the story of her experience, as told to Jennifer Leonard.*

For as long as I can remember, I've been smaller than other girls my age. Growing up in Washington, D.C., I never expected to be tall—my mom is 5'2", my dad is 5'8", and my brother and sister are short too—but I hated that people thought I was younger than I was. It got more annoying when I started college in New York City in September 2004. I was 18, 5'0", and 90 pounds. Once, at a store, a stranger actually asked me where my mother was! I was like, "Will people ever take me seriously?" I felt uncomfortable in my own skin.

Becoming a Decoy

Despite people commenting on my young looks, I loved being in New York. I was studying journalism and dance, but I also pursued another passion of mine—acting. And in February 2006, my sophomore year, I got my first TV job. The NBC show *Dateline* needed a girl who was over 18 but looked younger for a series called *To Catch a Predator* [TCAP]. I'd never seen it, but I loved that my look could work for me.

When producers sent me past episodes, I got a little scared. Basically, NBC and this organization called Perverted-Justice hire adult actors to pose as teens and chat with sexual predators online. When the predators show up to meet the "teen," police arrest them on camera. NBC hired me to be their first decoy, so I'd be on a Web cam pretending to be 13. It wasn't a typical acting gig, but I liked that I'd help put bad people in jail, so I took the job. My parents were worried, but producers assured us I'd be safe.

A month later, in March 2006, I flew to Ohio to start a four-day job. On the first day, I toured the "sting" house—a real house rigged with hidden cameras. I also sat in front of a Web cam while Perverted-Justice workers chatted with sexual predators online so it looked like I was the one chatting. Some men got so explicit, I was totally disgusted. These guys were 40 and trying to have sex with someone they thought was 13! I was instructed to make plans for them to come to the house. That's when I realized this wasn't just an acting job—I could be in real danger.

The next day, I watched on monitors as men entered the house expecting to find me. Instead, they met *Dateline*'s reporter, Chris Hansen. They looked horrified when they realized they'd been busted—then cops would arrest them. By the last day, we'd nabbed over 20 predators—and the producers decided to try something new. This time, they wanted me to be in the house to greet a guy. I was scared, but they told me what to say, and there were plenty of cops around if anything went wrong. When he knocked on the door, my heart was pounding! As I'd been trained, I said, "Come on in. I stubbed my toe and have to go get a Band-Aid, but I'll be right back." Then I ran upstairs. I started feeling guilty that this man's life was basically ruined—I was told he was a married teacher!

But when a producer reminded me that "early stage" predators like him often go on to commit other serious crimes, like rape, I stopped feeling bad.

I did two more stings, but soon predators started recognizing me from the show. I couldn't believe that after seeing the show, these guys were still trying to lure kids! NBC couldn't use me anymore—I was sad, but I also felt drained from the show and I was glad it was over.

I'm 20 now, and I'm pursuing an acting career. When I see an episode of TCAP, I have such respect for the decoys because I've been through it. I'm really grateful that my first acting job was exciting and meaningful.

Organizations to Contact

The editors have compiled the following list of organizations concerned with the issues debated in this book. The descriptions are derived from materials provided by the organizations. All have publications or information available for interested readers. The list was compiled on the date of publication of the present volume; the information provided here may change. Be aware that many organizations take several weeks or longer to respond to inquiries, so allow as much time as possible.

Association for the Treatment of Sexual Abusers (ATSA)
4900 SW Griffith Dr., Suite 274, Beaverton, OR   97005
(503) 643-1023 • fax: (503) 643-5084
e-mail: atsa@atsa.com
Web site: www.atsa.com

ATSA is an international nonprofit organization that was founded to foster research, facilitate informational exchange, further professional education, and provide for the advancement of professional standards and practices in the field of sex offender evaluation and treatment. ATSA aims to eliminate sexual victimization, protect communities, and prevent sexual assault through effective, responsible, and ethical treatment of sex offenders and to maintain high standards of professionalism and integrity within its membership. ATSA publishes numerous informational packages, position papers on public policies related to the treatment and management of sex offenders, book and video reviews, and the journal *Sexual Abuse: A Journal of Research and Treatment.*

Center for Sex Offender Management (CSOM)
c/o Center for Effective Public Policy, 8403 Colesville Rd.,
   Suite 720, Silver Spring, MD   20910
(301) 589-9383 • fax: (301) 589-3505

e-mail: askcsom@csom.org
Web site: www.csom.org

CSOM is a national project that supports state and local juris-
dictions in the effective management of sex offenders under
community supervision. CSOM's primary goal is to enhance
public safety by preventing further victimization through im-
proving the management of sex offenders in the community.
CSOM offers numerous publications on its Web site regarding
facts on sex offenders and sex offender management, public
policies, special offender populations, and offender treatment.

Darkness to Light
7 Radcliffe St., Suite 200, Charleston, SC   29403
(843) 965-5444 • fax: (843) 965-5449
e-mail: jschneider@d21.org
Web site: www.darkness2light.org

Darkness to Light is a national nonprofit organization and
initiative whose mission is to shift the responsibility for preventing child sexual abuse from children to adults, to reduce
child sexual abuse nationally through education and public
awareness aimed at adults, and to provide adults with information to prevent, recognize, and react responsibly to child
sexual abuse. Darkness to Light offers print and online educa-
tional resources to further its mission and conducts a sexual
abuse prevention training program for organizations and cor-
porations that serve children and youth.

Enough Is Enough (EIE)
746 Walker Rd., Suite 116, Great Falls, VA   22066
(888) 744-0004 • fax: (571) 333-5685
Web site: www.enough.org

Enough Is Enough, a nonpartisan, nonprofit organization, was
founded in 1994. The organization's goal is to make the Internet safer for children and families by confronting online pornography, child pornography, child stalking, and sexual preda-
tion with innovative initiatives and effective communications.

EIE communicates its message through television and other media and by conducting Internet safety seminars. The group also works with the legal community to enact legislation leading to a safer Internet.

GetNetWise/Interact Education Foundation
1634 Eye St. NW, Washington, DC   20009
e-mail: webmaster@getnetwise.org
Web site: www.getnetwise.org

GetNetWise is a project created by the Internet Education Foundation to help ensure that Internet users have safe and rewarding online experiences. Launched in 1999, GetNetWise was originally created in response to the recognition that people raising kids needed information and assistance in guiding children online. GetNetWise represents the collective efforts of a broad-based coalition of companies, public interest organizations, nonprofits, and trade associations all committed to empowering Internet users with tips, tutorials, and other interactive tools to keep their Internet experience positive, safe, and secure.

Katiesplace.org
e-mail: webmaster@wiredsafety.org
Web site: www.katiesplace.org

Katiesplace.org is a special program of WiredSafety.org, designed by and for young victims of Internet sexual exploitation and for those who love and care about them. The organization is named for Katie Tarbox, who was a victim of an Internet sexual predator when she was thirteen and wrote about her experience in the book *A Girl's Life Online*. The site includes true stories of victims and information for young people and educators. Its parent organization, WiredSafety-.org, sponsors a Cyber911 emergency tip line to help people know where to get help when they are being victimized online and to provide help when help is needed.

MaleSurvivor: The National Organization Against Male Sexual Victimization

PMB 103, 5505 Connecticut Ave. NW
Washington, DC 20015
(800) 738-4181
Web site: www.malesurvivor.org

MaleSurvivor provides resources and support for men who were sexually victimized as children, adolescents, or adults. The organization's mission is to advocate for male survivors, help healing, and prevent sexual abuse. Its Web site provides space for a number of discussion groups for survivors and professionals. The group also conducts Weekends of Recovery and holds conferences for its members.

National Center for Missing & Exploited Children (NCMEC) Charles B. Wang International Children's Bldg.

699 Prince St., Alexandria, Virginia 22314-3175
(703) 274-3900 • fax: (703) 274-2200
Web site: www.cybertipline.com

The National Center for Missing & Exploited Children was established in 1984 as a private, nonprofit organization to help prevent child abduction and sexual exploitation; help find missing children; and assist victims of child abduction and sexual exploitation, their families, and the professionals who serve them. The NCMEC operates a CyberTipline that the public may use to report Internet-related child sexual exploitation and distributes photographs and descriptions of missing children worldwide.

National Sexual Violence Resource Center (NSVRC)

123 N. Enola Dr., Enola, PA 17025
(717) 909-0710 • fax: (717) 909-0714
e-mail: resources@nsvrc.org
Web site: www.nsvrc.org

NSVRC is a national information and resource hub relating to all aspects of sexual violence. It is a project of the Pennsylvania Coalition Against Rape and is funded through a grant from the Centers for Disease Control and Prevention's Division of Violence Prevention. The NSVRC staff collects and disseminates a wide range of resources on sexual violence, including statistics, research, position statements, statutes, training curricula, prevention initiatives, and program information to assist coalitions, advocates, and others interested in understanding and eliminating sexual violence. NSVRC publishes a semiannual newsletter, the *Resource*; issues press releases and talking points on current events; and coordinates an annual national sexual assault awareness month (SAAM) campaign in April.

Rape, Abuse & Incest National Network (RAINN)
2000 L St. NW, Suite 406, Washington, DC   20036
(202) 544-1034 • fax: (202) 544-3556
e-mail: info@rainn.org
Web site: www.rainn.org

RAINN is a national anti-sexual-assault organization that operates, among its various programs, the National Sexual Assault Hotline, a nationwide partnership of more than eleven hundred local rape treatment hotlines to provide victims of sexual assault with free, confidential services around the clock. RAINN partners with numerous organizations to disseminate information about sexual assault prevention, recovery, and prosecution and is a frequent resource for television, radio, and print news outlets; local, state, and national policy makers; law enforcement; and rape treatment professionals on the issues related to rape and sexual assault. RAINN utilizes entertainment industry and community-based relationships to provide pamphlets to young women and men at concerts, on campus, and in communities.

SexualOffenders.com
1440 Coral Ridge Dr. #247, Coral Springs, FL   33071
(954) 827-0208 • fax: (954) 827-0133
e-mail: info@sexualoffenders.com
Web site: www.sexualoffenders.com

SexualOffenders.com is an informational Web site offering news about sexual abuse cases and links to state and county sex offender registries, sheriffs' offices, and news of sex crimes and related prosecution from around the world. The site also allows citizens to share information they have about criminal sex offenders, exchange links, and post comments in a blog-style format.

SOhopeful International
1900 NE 181st Ave., Suite 111, Portland, OR   97230
(212) 714-7061
e-mail: info@sohopeful.org
Web site: www.sohopeful.org

SOhopeful is an international civil rights organization focused on the human, civil, and constitutional rights of sex offenders and their families. SOhopeful does not condone or advocate abuse or excuse offenders. It encourages offenders to take personal responsibility, seek and participate in treatment, reunite with their families, and reintegrate into the community as active, contributing members of society. SOhopeful seeks to develop relationships with legislators who craft and approve laws dealing with penal codes, convey which provisions they oppose and support, and offer alternatives to existing laws mandating such activities as ongoing supervision and lifetime punishment of sex offenders. SOhopeful disseminates information to the public, treatment professionals, and legislators regarding research statistics on recidivism, risk levels, and the effects of registration and other public policies on offenders and their families.

Stop It Now!
351 Pleasant St., Suite B319, Northampton, MA   01060
(413) 587-3500 • fax: (413) 587-3505
e-mail: info@stopitnow.org
Web site: www.stopitnow.org

Stop It Now! is a national public health–based organization working to prevent child sexual abuse through educating adults—including those at risk for abusing and their families and friends—about the ways to prevent child sexual abuse and by promoting policy changes at local and national levels to support prevention strategies.

Survivors Network of those Abused by Priests (SNAP)
PO Box 6416, Chicago, IL   60680-6416
toll-free: (877) 762-7432
e-mail: snapclohessy@aol.com
Web site: www.snapnetwork.org

SNAP is a national support group—with no connections to church or church officials—offering confidential services for women and men victimized by religious authority figures such as priests, ministers, bishops, deacons, and nuns. SNAP offers support in person via monthly self-help group meetings in chapters across the country, over the phone, online, and at twice-a-year national meetings.

For Further Research

Books

Linda Lee Foltz, *Kids Helping Kids Break the Silence of Sexual Abuse*. Pittsburgh: Lighthouse Point, 2003.

R. Stephanie Good, *Exposed: The Harrowing Story of a Mother's Undercover Work with the FBI to Save Children from Internet Sex Predators*. Nashville: Thomas Nelson, 2007.

Mike Lew, *Victims No Longer: Men Recovering from Incest and Other Sexual Child Abuse*. New York: HarperCollins, 2004.

Cynthia Mather and Kristina Debye, *How Long Does It Hurt? A Guidebook to Recovering from Incest and Sexual Abuse for Teenagers, Their Friends, and Their Families*. San Francisco: Jossey-Bass, 2004.

Deanna S. Pledge, *When Something Feels Wrong: A Survival Guide About Abuse for Young People*. Minneapolis: Free Spirit, 2003.

Kerry Sheldon and Dennis Howitt, *Sex Offenders and the Internet*. Hoboken, NJ: Wiley, 2007.

Julian Sher, *Caught in the Web: Inside the Police Hunt to Rescue Children from Online Predators*. New York: Carroll & Graf, 2007.

Robin D. Stone, *No Secrets, No Lies: How Black Families Can Heal from Sexual Abuse*. New York: Broadway Books, 2004.

Periodicals

Charles Christopher, "Ain't I a Fool? A Victim of Clerical Sexual Abuse Looks Back," *America*, September 16, 2002.

Kevin Clarke, "Broken Trust, Broken Lives; Survivors of Priest Sexual Abuse Speak Out," *U.S. Catholic*, June 2002.

Geoffrey Douglas, "Jim McLaughlin's Secret War," *Yankee*, April 2002.

Cassidy Friedman, "Trolling for Online Predators," *Twin Falls (ID) Times-News*, September 13, 2006.

Ronnie Garrett, "Internet Watchdogs: Law Enforcers Go Online with Citizen Sleuths to Bring Internet Predators to Justice," *Law Enforcement Technology*, March 2007.

Jeff Harris, "Innocence Betrayed: Seeing a Trusted Teacher Being Convicted of Abuse Raises a Myriad of Emotions," *Maclean's*, December 20, 2004.

Margaret Magnarelli, "My Father Is an Internet Pervert," *Seventeen*, November 2003.

J. Scott Orr, "To Catch a Monster: Inside the Hunt for Online Predators," *Newark (NJ) StarLedger*, September 24, 2006.

People Weekly, "Kids with a Clue: Mary and Karen Teach FBI Agents How to Think, Act and Sound Just Like Teens—So They Can Help Catch Online Sexual Predators," September 15, 2003.

Kevin Poulsen, "MySpace Predator Caught by Code," *Wired*, October 16, 2006.

Mona H. Villarubia, "Forgive and Forget? Moving Closer to Forgiveness After Dallas," *America*, September 16, 2002.

Lee White, Diane White, and Bonnie Miller Rubin, "One Priest's Sin, One Couple's Suffering," *Ladies Home Journal, October 2002.*

Reed Williams and Amanda Codispoti, "He Had This Way About Him," *Roanoke (VA) Times*, November 19, 2006.

Index